A PASTORAL
ANSWERS
TO
QUESTIONS
ABOUT THE FAITH

Dedication

This book is dedicated to my father, Francis Patrick Bertolucci, who died December 4, 1994, age 84.

He now knows clearly the ultimate answer.

PASTORAL ANSWERS TO QUESTIONS ABOUT THE FAITH

Fr. John Patrick BERTOLUCCI

Our Sunday Visitor Publishing Division
Our Sunday Visitor, Inc.
Huntington, Indiana 46750

International Standard Book Number: 0-87973-749-2
Library of Congress Catalog Card Number: 94-68931

Cover design by Monica Watts

PRINTED IN THE UNITED STATES OF AMERICA

749

Contents

Foreword

Those who know me personally are aware of my dislike of being asked questions in a public forum, as if I were some kind of expert with the absolute and final answer on any topic. My attitude, subject to correction of course, comes from my sense of the awesomeness of truth and a humble recognition of the inadequacy of my finite human mind to grasp the completeness or complexity of any one issue. As Jesus said: "One among you is your Teacher, the rest are learners" (Mt 23:8, *NAB Catholic Edition*, Thomas Nelson: 1976).

It is as a "learner" that I share this book with you. When I lecture at Franciscan University of Steubenville in Ohio I tell my students: "An educated person is not one who has all the answers. An educated person is one who knows the One who is and has every answer." It is as a disciple of Jesus Christ and as an ordained servant-leader in his Church that I offer you, not complete, absolute, or final answers, but rather, the answers I have come to after prayer, reflection, and study, aided by my competent research assistant, Lisa Ferguson of Steubenville, Ohio, to whom I am deeply indebted.

As you make use of this book, my hope and prayer is that you, the reader, will likewise consider yourself a "learner" and a disciple of the only true teacher, the Lord Jesus Christ. My hope and prayer is that you will hear him speaking through the living and active teaching authority of the Catholic Church as found in our Pope and bishops. My hope and prayer is that you will discover, despite the human limitations of each of us, that there are answers and absolutes in Scripture and Tradition that can guide us and that are expressions of God's love for us.

We have not been left on our own to grope through life without wisdom and knowledge, direction and care. God is with us. God is with the Church. Jesus Christ is very much alive, and he is the source of all wisdom. He is the Ultimate Teacher and Final Word each human is seeking. For the service and good this publication may render, I give him praise and thanks.

"His [God's] *intent was that now, through the Church, the manifold wisdom of God should be made known to the rulers and authorities in the heavenly realms, according to his eternal purpose which he accomplished in Christ Jesus our Lord"* (Eph 3:10-11, *New International Version*).

Father John P. Bertolucci
Hudson, New York

Abbreviation Key to Biblical Books

In Alphabetical Order

Old Testament

Am	Amos	1 Kgs	1 Kings
Bar	Baruch	2 Kgs	2 Kings
1 Chr	1 Chronicles	Lam	Lamentations
2 Chr	2 Chronicles	Lv	Leviticus
Dn	Daniel	Mal	Malachi
Dt	Deuteronomy	1 Mc	1 Maccabees
Eccl	Ecclesiastes	2 Mc	2 Maccabees
Est	Esther	Mi	Micah
Ex	Exodus	Na	Nahum
Ez	Ezekiel	Neh	Nehemiah
Ezr	Ezra	Nm	Numbers
Gn	Genesis	Ob	Obadiah
Hb	Habakkuk	Prv	Proverbs
Hg	Haggai	Ps(s)	Psalms
Hos	Hosea	Ru	Ruth
Is	Isaiah	Sg	Song of Solomon
Jb	Job	Sir	Sirach
Jdt	Judith	1 Sm	1 Samuel
Jer	Jeremiah	2 Sm	2 Samuel
Jgs	Judges	Tb	Tobit
Jl	Joel	Wis	Wisdom
Jon	Jonah	Zec	Zechariah
Jos	Joshua	Zep	Zephaniah

New Testament

Act	Acts of the Apostles	Mk	Mark
Col	Colossians	Mt	Matthew
1 Cor	1 Corinthians	Phil	Philippians
2 Cor	2 Corinthians	Phlm	Philemon
Eph	Ephesians	1 Pt	1 Peter
Gal	Galatians	2 Pt	2 Peter
Heb	Hebrews	Rom	Romans
Jas	James	Rv	Revelation
Jn	John	1 Thes	1 Thessalonians
1 Jn	1 John	2 Thes	2 Thessalonians
2 Jn	2 John	Ti	Titus
3 Jn	3 John	1 Tm	1 Timothy
Jude	Jude	2 Tm	2 Timothy
Lk	Luke		

Chapter I: The Sacraments

Q A Protestant friend told me that he was baptized only in the name of Jesus, and he quoted a verse from Acts to prove his baptism's validity. Why does the Catholic Church baptize in the name of the Father, Son, and Holy Spirit?

A In Acts 2:38-39, the apostle Peter urged the Jews to be "baptized ... in the name of Jesus Christ" to receive the forgiveness of sins and the outpouring of the Holy Spirit. In Matthew 28:19 Jesus instructed the apostles to baptize new converts "in the name of the Father, and of the Son, and of the Holy Spirit."

According to Scripture scholars, it is likely that in the early Church both formulas were used in initiating new converts into a relationship with Jesus Christ and into the Christian community. As the Church continued under the inspiration of the Holy Spirit, the normative formula gradually became the one specifying the Father, Son, and Holy Spirit. That formula affirms the actual nature of the Trinity, and it incorporates the content of the shorter formula.

Jesus' own baptism serves as a sign to us of the action of the Father, Son, and Holy Spirit in Christian baptism: "When all the people were baptized, and Jesus was at prayer after likewise being baptized, the skies opened, and the Holy Spirit descended on him in visible form like a dove. A voice from heaven was heard to say: 'You are my beloved Son. On you my favor rests' " (Lk 3:21-22).

Q Though I was raised in a Catholic home, I stopped going to Mass after I committed a sin that I know God will not forgive. Recently, however, I've had an increasing desire to receive the Eucharist, but the thought of that sin holds me back. Could God ever forgive me after what I did?

A The Lord does not want you to feel condemned because of a sin in your past. He is infinitely loving, and as we repent from our sins and ask his forgiveness, he forgives us. He no longer holds those sins against us. When we confess our sins, and this includes *any* sins in our lives, God who is just will forgive us our sins and cleanse us from all iniquity (see 1 Jn 1:9). Read over Psalm 51, and ask the Lord to allow you to experience his healing forgiveness.

It is important that you speak to a priest and ask to receive the sacrament of reconciliation. The Lord uses this sacrament as a channel of his love and the ordinary means for receiving forgiveness. Confession helps us to be assured of his forgiveness and to receive spiritual care and counsel on living a holy life.

Let me also assure you that the Lord Jesus Christ loves you intimately and has called you by name to be his very own (see Is 43:1). Although he is the Son of God, Jesus chose to humble himself, become a human being, and suffer upon the cross to save us from hopelessness and sin. Jesus longs for all of us to be in a personal relationship with him and to know his healing love and forgiveness. Only he can free us from our sins and heal the hurts of life.

It is my hope and prayer that you will come to experience Jesus' infinite love for you and ask him to come into your life as your Lord, Savior, and Healer. He is the Rock upon which you can build your life, and in him and in his Church, you can live a holy and joyful life.

Q If Jesus commanded us to eat his Body and drink his Blood, why is it that at most Masses Holy Communion is offered only under the species of bread?

A Communion under the forms of both bread and wine was the norm for many centuries in the Church. Gradually, mostly because of its convenience, the use of bread only became universal. Though this practice may seem to contradict Jesus' words, the Catholic Church has always taught that the Body and Blood, soul and divinity of Jesus Christ are received even under one form only. Thus, if you receive the eucharistic bread only, you are receiving the whole and entire Christ.

One of the reforms recommended by the Second Vatican Council was a return to Communion under both species. According to *Sacrosanctum Concilium,* "Constitution on the Sacred Liturgy," "Communion under both kinds may be granted when the bishops think fit … in cases to be determined by the Apostolic See" (No. 55).

The *General Instruction on the Roman Missal* (1969) states, "The meaning of Communion is signified as clearly as possible when it is given under both kinds. In this form the meal-aspect of the Eucharist is more fully manifested, and Christ's intention that the new and eternal covenant ratified in his blood is better expressed. Also the connection between the eucharistic meal and the heavenly banquet in the Father's kingdom becomes easier to see" (No. 240).

The application of this teaching varies in the Church. In the parish I serve, the congregation always receives Communion under both species. Some churches do this only on special occasions. The communicant always has the option to receive Communion under the form of bread alone.

I'd advise you to read *This Holy and Living Sacrifice: Directory for the Celebration and Reception of Communion Under Both Kinds.* It is available from the United States Catholic Conference, Office of Publishing Services (1-800-235-USCC).

Q A friend of mine was not married in the Catholic Church because her first marriage was not annulled. Our priest permits her to receive Communion. Is he allowed to do that?

A No. The Catholic Church forbids remarriage after divorce unless one's first marriage has been annulled. If one remarries without the Church's blessing, one may not partake of Holy Communion.

Some priests disagree with this teaching, so they allow divorced and invalidly remarried Catholics to receive Communion. In encouraging others to abandon the Church's teaching, they undermine the Church's teaching on the dignity, sacred value, and permanence of marriage. Only if the couple agrees to a brother-sister relationship may they receive Communion.

While sacramental participation is denied divorced and invalidly remarried Catholics, they may still attend Mass and other Church-related activities, have their children baptized, and raise them in the Catholic faith. Divorced Catholics who: 1) have *not* remarried, or 2) who have had their marriage annulled before remarrying within the Church, or 3) who remain single after obtaining an annulment may continue to fully participate in the sacramental life of the Church.

Since this issue is a delicate, personal one, it may be advisable to talk to your priest to obtain further wisdom. You may not know all the details of your friend's situation.

Q My great aunt has had major surgery twice in the last year. Both times I tried to convince her to receive the sacrament of the anointing of the sick. She refused even to consider it, saying it was only for the dying, and she's not dying. What should I say next time she's seriously ill?

A You are right to try to prepare your great aunt to receive the anointing of the sick. But perhaps you'd get a better hearing now than the next time she's ill. She may be more open to your explanation when she's not in the midst of a health crisis.

The mistaken idea that the anointing of the sick is the sacrament for the dying remains prevalent today, even though Vatican II documents and changes in the rite since the Council have manifested the sacrament's healing nature more clearly. Pope Paul VI's "Apostolic Constitution on the Sacrament of the Anointing of the Sick" (1972) traces the New Testament and early Church teachings, which consistently associate the sacrament with healing. The Pope quotes the Council of Trent: " 'The central reality is the grace of the Holy Spirit. The anointing removes any remaining sin and its remnants. It brings relief and strength to the soul of sick persons, making them greatly confident in the divine mercy. Thus sustained, they can more easily bear their illness, be better able to withstand the temptations of the devil in ambush (Gn 3:15), and sometimes they regain bodily strength, if this will contribute to the health of the soul.' "

He also quotes the "Constitution on the Sacred Liturgy," which says it "is not a sacrament for those only who are at the point of death. Hence, as soon as any one of the faithful begins to be in danger of death from sickness or old age, the fitting time for him to receive this sacrament has certainly already arrived" (No. 73).

The focus of the present rite, as described in the "Introduction to the Rite of Anointing and to the Pastoral Care of the Sick" (1972) is the total health of the individual, the healing of the soul overflowing into the healing of the body. Noting that seriously ill people have special need for divine grace, the document states, "The sacrament gives to the sick person the grace of the Holy Spirit by which the whole person is made healthy, is encouraged to trust in God, and is given the strength to resist the temptations of the Evil One and avoid succumbing to anxiety about death" (No. 6). It continues, "Restoration to health may follow the reception of the sacrament if this will be in the interests of the sick person's salvation" (No. 7).

Those to be anointed include those who are seriously ill; elderly people if they are weak, though not dangerously ill; those about to undergo surgery necessitated by a serious illness; and children who are mature enough to be comforted by the sacrament (see *Pastoral Care of the Sick*, Nos. 9-12).

As a hospital chaplain, I have personally witnessed the peace and consolation this sacramental ministry brings to the sick and elderly. I have also been awed by the medically unexplainable recoveries made by some who were clinically near death and who, in my opinion, miraculously recuperated after being anointed. I have also appreciated the reality of those who die in peace after receiving the sacrament. Death in Christ is the ultimate healing.

 Why do so few Catholics go to confession these days?

A The bishops of the Church, in union with Pope John Paul II, admit that the sacrament of penance is in crisis. Meeting in synod to discuss this issue the bishops spoke of "the obscuring of the moral and religious conscience, the lessening of a sense of sin, the distortion of the concept of repentance, and the lack of effort to live an authentically Christian life" (Pope John Paul II, *Penance and Reconciliation*, No. 28). The bishops also speak of a "sometimes widespread idea that one can obtain forgiveness directly from God, even in an habitual way, without approaching the sacrament of reconciliation" (*Penance and Reconciliation*, No. 28).

I also think many Catholics have not matured in their faith beyond a childhood approach of confessing a "grocery list" of sins and are reluctant to bring up before the priest deep personal areas of sin and weakness, preferring to listen to the attitudes of secular society and popular psychology that certain activities, especially of a sexual nature, are "normal" and "common" so they are not gravely sinful. A current emphasis on "social sin" has also replaced a previous emphasis on "personal sin," so many Catholics are confused as to just what must be confessed and what seriously violates the covenant we have been called into as God's people.

The real problem, I sense, is that many Catholics are ignoring the moral mandates of Scripture and the Magisterium of the Church, preferring to accept more liberal and popular teachings as if they were equal in authority to the word of God. This is clearly a terrible mistake, as the teachings of the word of God, which include the magisterial instructions of our Pope and bishops, are the primary source of formation of conscience. We learn the mandates of the new covenant from Scripture and Tradition. These are the norms we are to live by. More attention and assent must be given to the teachings coming from our Pope and bishops in forming a correct conscience in matters of faith and morals. The apostolic teaching office is God's gift to us, so we may remain on a holy and healthy path of life.

Q I had never seen a baby baptized by immersion until my grandson was baptized last month. Is immersion really permissible in the Catholic Church? It looks so unsafe.

A The *Code of Canon Law* states, "Baptism is to be conferred either by immersion or by pouring" (Canon 854). Immersion is the preferred form, and according to the official baptismal ritual of the Church, it is a more suitable symbol of participation in the Death and Resurrection of Christ. Renovated and newly built churches will now have to provide for this manner of baptizing children and adults.

I find it a joy to see babies baptized by immersion. Gently immersing the infant in warm water and lifting him or her out again dramatically symbolizes the truth that St. Paul wrote about in Romans: "Are you not aware that we who were baptized into Christ Jesus were baptized into his death? Through baptism into his death we were buried with him, so that, just as Christ was raised from the dead by the glory of the Father, we too might live a new life" (6:3, 4).

Of the many children I have seen baptized by immersion, none has suffered any ill effects. It is a very safe practice, and I recommend it, unless for health reasons it would be inadvisable.

Q Why do we have to confess our sins to a priest?

A When Jesus chose his apostles to minister to the people, he gave them a share in his power to preach the good news, heal, and cast out demons. After his Resurrection, he shared with them the power to forgive sins: "Then he breathed on them and said: 'Receive the Holy Spirit. If you forgive men's sins, they are forgiven them; if you hold them bound, they are held bound' " (Jn 20:22-23). The Catholic Church believes bishops are successors to the apostles. They share their apostolic authority to forgive sins with priests. They exercise this authority on behalf of the Church community, the family of God, and in the name of our triune God.

Surely Jesus knew the deep need of humans to hear words of assurance and to have others with whom the most serious of burdens could be shared. The sacrament of penance or reconciliation ministers to the whole person — spiritually, psychologically, and physically. We can benefit not only from the forgiveness experienced but also from the counsel given by a priest-confessor.

The Catholic Church also recognizes that when we sin we not only offend God, we also offend the family of God. The priest has been appointed a minister of reconciliation representing both Jesus Christ and the community of Christ, acting in the name of and on behalf of the body of Christ, the

Church. This truth is what gives life and efficacy to our whole sacramental system instituted by Christ.

I recommend confession once a month for anyone who truly hungers and thirsts for holiness. Where priests are taking this ministry seriously and making themselves available to minister this healing sacrament and where the full and authentic gospel is being proclaimed, there is a definite increase in the number of penitents availing themselves of the sacrament.

Q Do you know of any good inspirational study guides on the Eucharist?

A First, I recommend the Vatican II document, "Constitution on the Sacred Liturgy" (*Sacrosanctum Concilium*), which discusses the Eucharist in light of the sacrifice of the Mass. I believe all Catholics should read the documents of Vatican II for a foundational understanding of Catholic Church teaching. Here are some other good books on the Eucharist:

The Holy Eucharist by St. Alphonsus Liguori is considered a classic. It is available by writing to Victory Mission, R.R. #2, Box 25, Brookings, South Dakota 57006 or by calling (605) 693-3983.

Living Eucharist: Counter-Sign to Our Age and Answer to Crisis by Father George W. Kosicki, C.S.B., is an inspirational book about the mystery of the Eucharist. It may be ordered from the Shrine of the Divine Mercy by calling (413) 298-3931.

The Holy Eucharist (Ignatius) by Father Aidan Nichols, O.P., which looks at how the theology of the Holy Eucharist developed and what it means for us today, is another good resource. For an Ignatius Press catalog, call (914) 835-4216.

Corpus Christi: An Encyclopedia of the Eucharist (Liturgical Press) by Father Michael O'Carroll, C.S.Sp., is an excellent reference. It is available through Theological Book Service, 1-800-558-0580.

Q Why are we absolved of our sins before we do the penance prescribed by our confessor?

A "Satisfaction" or "penance" was required before absolution in the older tradition. Public penance was even required before certain mortal sins could be forgiven. Over time the manner in which the sacrament was celebrated changed, and the act of satisfaction or penance was postponed until after absolution.

Catholic doctrine and practice today are expressed in the *Rite of Penance of the Roman Ritual*:

"True conversion is completed by expiation for the sins committed, by amendment of life, and also by rectifying injuries done.... Therefore, it is necessary that the act of penance really be a remedy for sin and a help to renewal of life. Thus penitents, 'forgetting the things that are behind' (Phil 3:13) again become part of the mystery of salvation and press on to the things that are to come" (No. 6).

"The priest imposes an act of penance or expiation on the penitent; this should serve not only as atonement for past sins but also as an aid to new life and an antidote for weakness. As far as possible, therefore, the penance should correspond to the seriousness and nature of the sins. This act of penance may suitably take the form of prayer, self-denial, and especially service to neighbor and works of mercy. These will underline the fact that sin and its forgiveness have a social aspect" (No. 18).

Q I was baptized in the Holy Spirit about a year ago. Do I still need to be confirmed?

A Yes. Though the baptism in the Holy Spirit gives us a deeper personal experience of the Holy Spirit's presence and an awareness of his gifts and actions in our lives, it is not a replacement for the sacrament of confirmation.

As Catholics we believe that what some prefer to call "the release of the Holy Spirit" helps us to better appreciate and assimilate the graces available to us through the sacramental system of our Church. In the *Code of Canon Law*, the Catholic Church teaches that the sacraments, actions of Christ and the Church, are "signs and means by which the faith is expressed and strengthened, worship is rendered to God, and the sanctification of humankind is effected" (Canon 840).

Canon 842 says, "The sacraments of baptism, confirmation, and the Most Holy Eucharist are so interrelated that they are required for full Christian initiation." And in Canon 879, we read: "The sacrament of confirmation impresses a character and by it the baptized, continuing on the path of Christian initiation, are enriched by the gift of the Holy Spirit and bound more perfectly to the Church; it strengthens them and obliges them more firmly to be witnesses to Christ by word and deed and to spread and defend the faith."

Thus, while you may feel more of the power of the Holy Spirit in your life already, because you are a member of Christ's Church, you will want the ecclesial graces and added blessings that come from the laying on of hands by the bishop of your diocese, the ordinary minister of confirmation.

Finally, for further enlightenment, I recommend *Christian Initiation and Baptism in the Holy Spirit* (Liturgical Press) by Fathers Kilian McDonnell, O.S.B., and George Montague, S.M., and its summary booklet *Fanning the Flame*.

 Where in the Bible does it say that we are saved by baptism?

A There are many biblical references to the necessity of baptism for salvation.

Jesus clearly stated this to Nicodemus: "No one can enter

into God's kingdom without being begotten of water and Spirit" (Jn 3:5). Another reference is found in Jesus' final instructions to the disciples before his Ascension: "Go into the whole world and proclaim the good news to all creation. The man who believes in it and accepts baptism will be saved" (Mk 16:15-16; see also Mt 28:19).

The need of baptism for salvation is frequently stated in the book of Acts and the New Testament letters: "Peter answered: 'You must reform and be baptized, each one of you, in the name of Jesus Christ, that your sins may be forgiven; then you will receive the gift of the Holy Spirit' " (Acts 2:38; you may also want to look up these references: Acts 2:41; 8:12-13, 16, 36, 38; 9:18; 10:47; 19:3-5; Rom 6:3; 1 Cor 12:13).

The *New Catholic Encyclopedia* (Vol. 2, McGraw-Hill) has an excellent article entitled "Baptism in the Bible," which deals with the Old Testament roots of baptism as well as baptism in the New Testament.

Q Is the Communion host that is consumed by the priest any different from the smaller hosts consumed by the congregation at Mass? Does the larger host used by the priest mean anything?

A The *General Instruction on the Roman Missal* stipulates that the bread used in the celebration of Mass should have the appearance of real food and be made in such a way that the priest is able to break it into parts and distribute them to at least some of those participating (see No. 283). Thus, the main host is usually large enough to be broken for distribution and to be seen when held at the elevation for adoration by the people.

The size of the Communion host is irrelevant to the Real Presence of the Lord. Each particle and each portion of the consecrated bread is substantially the Body, Blood, soul, and divinity of Jesus Christ. What is important, however, is that one host be large enough to be visibly broken for distribution. This part of the Communion rite is called the "breaking of the bread."

In apostolic times, this very gesture of Christ at the Last Supper gave the entire eucharistic action its name. This rite is not merely functional, but is a sign that in the sharing of the one Bread of Life, which is Christ, we who are many are made one body (see 1 Cor 10:17).

You may also be interested to learn that Church law requires that the bread be made of wheat alone and made recently enough that there is no danger of corruption. Unleavened bread is to be used in the Latin Church (see *Code of Canon Law*, Canons 924, 926). It is usually round in shape, but that is more by custom than by requirement.

Q There seem to be fewer Catholics going to confession these days, yet practically everyone in our parish goes to Communion. Is this acceptable to the Church?

A I believe you rightly sense a problem here. The clear teaching of the Catholic Church as proclaimed in the instructions of our recent popes and in Church law is that "no one who is conscious of being in mortal sin, however contrite he may believe himself to be, is to approach the Holy Eucharist without having first made a sacramental confession. If this person finds himself in need and has no means of going to confession, he should first make an act of perfect contrition" (Pope John Paul II, *Reconciliation and Penance*, No. 27).

Catholic doctrine clearly teaches that "the sacrament of penance is the ordinary way of obtaining forgiveness and the remission of serious sins committed after baptism" (*Reconciliation and Penance*, No. 31). The Church admits that Christ can minister his saving and forgiving love outside and above the sacraments but that he himself "desired and provided that the simple and precious sacraments of faith would ordinarily be the effective means through which his redemptive power passes and operates" (*Reconciliation and Penance*, No. 31). It is foolish and presumptuous to ignore confession to a priest, especially when one is in serious sin.

The bishops of the United States have expressed their concern over Communion being received without the proper dispositions. Their official teaching is now available in most of the missalettes used in our churches. It states in part: "In order to be disposed properly to receive Communion, communicants should not be conscious of grave sin, have fasted for an hour, and seek to live in charity and love with their neighbors. Persons conscious of grave sin must first be reconciled with God and the Church through the sacrament of penance. A frequent reception of the sacrament of penance is encouraged for all."

I am so pleased to see a revival in the use of confession in many parts of the country, as at Franciscan University of Steubenville, where priests are available six days of the week. In the parish I live in, we are experiencing an increase in the use of that most-needed sacrament as we preach and teach the authentic and full doctrine of the Catholic Church. It would be well for all of us to read and prayerfully reflect upon the tradition expressed in 1 Corinthians 11:23-34.

Q I know that deacons, priests, and bishops are all ordained. How is one ordination different from another?

A The Catholic Church teaches that " 'the divinely instituted ecclesiastical ministry is exercised in different degrees by those who even from ancient times have been called bishops, priests, and deacons' ... there are two degrees of ministerial participation in the priesthood of Christ: the episcopacy and the presbyterate. The diaconate is intended to help and serve them" (*Catechism of the Catholic Church*, No. 1554).

All three degrees are conferred by ordination, a "sacramental act which integrates a man into the order of bishops, presbyters, or deacons, and goes beyond a simple election, designation, delegation, or institution by the community, for it confers a gift of the Holy Spirit that permits the exercise of a 'sacred power' which can come only from Christ himself through his Church" (*Catechism*, No. 1538).

In all three degrees, Holy Orders consists primarily in the bishop's laying on of hands and solemn prayer of consecration "asking God for the outpouring of the Holy Spirit and his gifts proper to the ministry to which the candidate is being ordained" (*Catechism*, No. 1573).

The ordination of a bishop " 'confers, together with the office of sanctifying, also the offices of teaching and ruling.... In fact ... by the imposition of hands and through the words of the consecration, the grace of the Holy Spirit is given, and a sacred character is impressed in such wise that bishops, in an eminent and visible manner, take the place of Christ himself, teacher, shepherd, and priest, and act as his representative.' 'By virtue, therefore, of the Holy Spirit who has been given to them, bishops have been constituted true and authentic teachers of the faith and have been made pontiffs and pastors' " (*Catechism*, No. 1558).

Priests, coworkers of the bishops, " 'are consecrated in order to preach the gospel and shepherd the faithful as well as to celebrate divine worship as true priests of the New Testament' " (*Catechism*, No. 1564).

Deacons receive the imposition of hands " 'not unto priesthood, but unto the ministry' " (*Catechism*, No. 1569). "It is the task of deacons to assist the bishop and priests in the celebration of the divine mysteries, above all the Eucharist, in the distribution of Holy Communion, in assisting at and blessing marriages, in the proclamation of the gospel and preaching, in presiding over funerals, and in dedicating themselves to the various ministries of charity" (*Catechism*, No. 1570).

Chapter II: Moral Problems

Q Some friends of mine go to a church that forbids its members to drink alcoholic beverages. What does the Bible teach about the use of alcohol?

A Although some Christian traditions are against any consumption of alcohol (including wine at Communion), it is clear in both the Old and New Testaments that wine was a very common drink of those who loved and followed the Lord.

The Catholic Church understands Scripture on the subject this way: In and of itself, alcohol is not sinful.

It is, however, a sin to allow ourselves to become intoxicated or to lose control of our senses because of alcohol (see Eph 5:18). As it says in Romans 13:13, "Let us live honorably as in daylight; not in carousing and drunkenness." The Lord calls us not to be influenced by the society around us but to be holy and set apart for his honor (see Rom 12:1-2; Eph 4:24; 1 Jn 2:16-17).

The Lord sometimes calls individuals, as he did St. John the Baptist, to abstain from all alcoholic drinks (see Lk 1:15). Also, in recent years we've become aware of the great damage alcohol can do through its addictive properties. Most families know firsthand the misery caused by alcoholism. You should keep these considerations in mind as you seek the Lord about how you should approach alcohol.

Q Why is there a loss of the sense of sin in our society today?

A The moral conscience of a people can become seriously clouded. In *Reconciliation and Penance*, Pope John Paul II quotes Pope Pius XII, who declared: "The sin of the century is the loss of the sense of sin" (No. 18). John Paul II maintained that this is due to a deepening "secularism" in our world, described as "a movement of ideas and behavior which advocates a humanism totally without God, completely centered upon the cult of action and production and caught up in the heady enthusiasm of consumerism and pleasure-seeking, unconcerned with the danger of 'losing one's soul' "(No. 18).

Indeed man can attempt to build a world without God, but we have already seen clearly in the historic events of these past years that such a world "will end by turning against [man]" (No. 18). Another reason Pope John Paul II gives for a loss of the sense of sin "is to be found in the errors made in evaluating certain findings of the human sciences" (No. 18).

I have found this to be true in my pastoral work. There is a heightened concern on the part of many professional people "to avoid creating feelings of guilt or to place limits on freedom." All failings are blamed on "society" and the individual is no longer held responsible.

Another reason for the loss of a sense of sin is called "moral relativism" wherein there is a denial of absolute and unconditional values and intrinsically illicit acts. Everything is reduced to subjective opinion and personal feelings, and there are no objective norms and commandments.

I think another major reason for a loss of sense of sin is a "loss of sense of God." Our sense of what is right and wrong and our sense of sin and virtue is directly related to our experience of the true God as revealed in and through Jesus Christ.

Clearly the need for evangelization is obvious, both in the world and in the Church.

Q What's the difference between making a good examination of conscience and scrupulosity? It seems to me that you have to be scrupulous to make a good confession.

A An examination of conscience is a spiritual exercise that helps prepare us for the sacrament of penance. Guided by the Holy Spirit, we take an honest look at ourselves to evaluate how we've sinned against God and against one another in thought, word, or deed, and where we need to grow in virtue.

Scrupulosity, in its current, popular definition of being careful or exact, can indeed aid us in discovering and correcting our faults. But, when scrupulosity is "the habit of imagining sin where none exists, or grave sin where the matter is venial" (John A. Hardon, S.J., *Modern Catholic Dictionary*, Doubleday, 1980), confusion and doubt rather than clarity and contrition result.

According to the *New Catholic Encyclopedia* (Vol. 12, McGraw-Hill) scruples may be temporary or chronic, mild or severe, limited or almost boundless in extent, and can render a person incapable of making the daily decisions of life: "Decisions require a disproportionate amount of time and energy, and are always accompanied by feelings of guilt and doubt. Never at peace, the mind compulsively reexamines and reevaluates every aspect of a matter about which scruples center. With increasing doubts and mounting fear, the mind is so blinded and confused that volitional activity becomes difficult or impossible.... There is a more or less constant, unreasonable, and morbid fear of sin, error, and guilt."

A variety of things can cause scruples, including poor physical health, certain psychological conditions, or an erroneous conscience. Thus, in some cases improved physical health or, through instruction, helping the person form a correct conscience, can alleviate or eliminate the problem. When the root is psychological, however, a confessor may recommend that the person seek additional assistance from a mental-health professional. There are some new psychiatric medications that have been very helpful to those with severe cases of scrupulosity. But, most of all, confessors must try to bring people who suffer from scrupulosity to an experience of the mercy of God. As the Lord told Blessed Faustina Kowalska, "Let the weak, sinful soul have no fear to approach me, for even if it had more sins than there are grains of sand in the world, all will be drowned in the unmeasurable depths of my mercy."

Q My husband became a Catholic twelve years ago, but is now attending a nondenominational church. He keeps nagging me to leave the Catholic Church and makes fun of Catholic beliefs that he now sees as contradicting Scripture. What can I do?

A I think prayer should be your first defense. Ask the Holy Spirit to touch your husband's mind and heart and reveal to him the truth contained in Catholic Church teaching. Pray for yourself, for the gifts of wisdom, love, and patience in the midst of this trying situation.

If possible, seek emotional and spiritual support from a close friend or from your prayer group. You may also want to talk to your confessor about it.

I believe it would be appropriate to let your husband know how much you love the Catholic Church and how strongly you feel about remaining Catholic. Also, share with him how hurt you are when he makes fun of the beliefs you hold dear. Tell him you'd be happy to discuss your differences if he'd be willing to do so in a respectful manner.

You could offer to study the teachings of the Catholic Church with him. He may be surprised to find out what the Catholic Church really teaches.

Dr. Alan Schreck's *Catholic and Christian* (Servant) explains some of the Catholic beliefs other Christians have difficulty understanding.

Two other good resources (don't let the similarity of the names confuse you) are Our Sunday Visitor's *The Catholic Answer Book*, by Father Peter Stravinskas, and Catholic Answers, an apologetics and evangelization organization with a catalog of fine books, tapes, and tracts on defending the Catholic faith.

To order the book, call 1-800-348-2440. To order the Catholic Answers catalog call (619) 541-1131, or write P.O. Box 17490, San Diego, California 92177. Remember, God can make this too "work together for the good" (Rom 8:28).

Q I am a correctional officer in a medium-security male facility. Can I carry out my duties, even when physical force is sometimes needed to keep order and maintain security, and be a Spirit-filled Catholic Christian too?

A The Catholic Church has long taught that it is permissible for a government to restrain those whose behavior threatens the rights of its citizens. Turn to your Bible and read Romans 13:1-7. For those in a position of authority, the infliction of penalties upon violators of the law or the use of reasonable force to control inappropriate behavior is morally acceptable.

The section of the *Catechism of the Catholic Church* entitled "Legitimate Defense," addresses your concerns: "Legitimate defense can be not only a right but a grave duty for someone responsible for another's life, the common good of the family, or of the state" (No. 2265).

It continues, "Preserving the common good of society requires rendering the aggressor unable to inflict harm. For this reason the traditional teaching of the Church has acknowledged as well-founded the right and duty of legitimate public authority to punish malefactors by means of penalties commensurate with the gravity of the crime ... those holding authority have the right to repel by armed force aggressors against the community in their charge" (No. 2266).

Your attitude in carrying out your duties is very important. The use of physical force becomes unjust when it is done out of malice or an unwillingness to forgive. As a Christian you are obliged to maintain an attitude of charity toward your prisoners for as the *Catechism* notes, "Punishment has a medicinal value; as far as possible it should contribute to the correction of the offender" (No. 2266).

As a chaplain at two correctional facilities, I have seen how important it is for correctional officers to have a Christian attitude and posture toward those who are incarcerated. I would like to see more Christians working in our prisons.

Q As a Catholic and a nursing instructor at a state university, I feel an obligation to tell my students the truth about abortion. As nurses, they will be confronted with the abortion issue many times during their careers. My dilemma is that I can't directly convey my Christian values without jeopardizing my job. What can I do?

A You may not be allowed to address the abortion issue from a Catholic view in the classroom, but when students ask for your views privately you can still strongly articulate your stand against the atrocity of abortion. You can make it clear that abortion is the killing of innocent human life, which is sacred to the Lord. At the same time, you can also express God's loving forgiveness for those who are sorry for having had abortions and his desire to heal them of the emotional, physical, and psychological scars of abortion. You can make various pro-life pamphlets available to interested students and offer to speak personally to anyone who would like to hear your views in more detail.

Presenting the *medical* arguments against abortion as part of your course material is another avenue open to you. Many people never hear about the physical, emotional, and psychological damage caused by abortion until they experience it personally. *Abortion: Questions and Answers* (Hayes Publishing Co.) by Dr. and Mrs. J.C. Willke contains information on that aspect of the abortion issue.

Q What is the Catholic Church's teaching on using foul or obscene language?

A The Catholic Church does not have a list of obscene words or expressions that should be avoided or a specific official teaching on right speech. In Scripture and the writings of the saints, however, there are plenty of guidelines about purity of speech.

I strongly believe that as Christians we should strive to eliminate from our speech any words or expressions that dishonor God or in any way undermine the essential dignity of another human being or group or class of human beings.

Here is some of what Scripture tells us about purity of speech:

"You shall not take the name of the Lord, your God, in vain. For the Lord will not leave unpunished him who takes his name in vain" (Ex 20:7).

"As for lewd conduct or promiscuousness or lust of any sort, let them not even be mentioned among you; your holiness forbids this. Nor should there be any obscene, silly, or suggestive talk; all that is out of place.... There was a time when you were darkness, but now you are light in the Lord. Well, then, live as children of light" (Eph 5:3, 4, 8).

"Put to death whatever in your nature is rooted in earth ... all the anger and quick temper, the malice, the insults, the foul language.... Whatever you do, whether in speech or in action, do it in the name of the Lord Jesus" (Col 3:5, 8, 17).

Another important passage is James 3:1-12, in which the author talks about restraining the tongue. It says, in part, "The tongue no man can tame. It is a restless evil, full of deadly poison. We use it to say, 'Praised be the Lord and Father'; then we use it to curse men, though they are made in the likeness of

God. Blessing and curse come out of the same mouth. This ought not to be, my brothers! Does a spring gush forth fresh water and foul from the same outlet?"

In the writings of the saints, too, we find many words of wisdom about right speech: St. John Bosco once said, "No matter how good food is, if poison is mixed with it, it may cause the death of him who eats it. So it is with conversation. A single bad word, an evil action, an unbecoming joke, is often enough to harm one or more young listeners, and may later on cause them to lose God's grace."

St. Francis de Sales had this to say in his *Introduction to the Devout Life*: "Be careful never to let an indecent word leave your lips, for even if you do not speak with an evil intention those who hear it may take it in a different way. An evil word falling into a weak heart grows and spreads like a drop of oil on a piece of linen cloth. Sometimes it seizes the heart in such a way as to fill it with a thousand unclean thoughts and temptations."

I think Scripture and the witness of the saints make it clear that as Christians we must not offend God or cause scandal to others by improper speech.

Q I had a tubal ligation after the birth of my younger child. Since then, my husband and I have been studying Catholic Church teachings and are trying to decide if we should become Catholics. Now that I know the Church's teaching on contraception I am wondering if my sterilization is a barrier to becoming Catholic. What do you think?

A Your tubal ligation is no impediment to becoming a Catholic. I encourage you, however, to mention it to the priest (along with other concerns of your life that may be a source of guilt) when the moment comes for you to make your first confession as a Catholic.

Enter the Church knowing the mercy and forgiveness of the Lord.

Chapter III: The Church

Q Excommunication seems like one of those medieval practices that should have been reformed by the Second Vatican Council. Is there still such a thing as excommunication in the modern Church?

A Indeed there is! The Church is a sign of the kingdom of God and as such must maintain a certain standard of morality and right order. While we are primarily a faith community of love and service, we cannot afford to ignore significant violations of faith and order. People who join our Church have a right to expect to find a reasonably well-defined community. Today we characteristically speak of plurality and diversity within the Church. True orthodoxy can admit of such. However, there are boundaries that we cannot cross and still consider ourselves Catholic Christians.

Book VI of the 1983 *Code of Canon Law*, which now governs the Catholic Church, is devoted to the topic of "Sanctions in the Church." Canon 1311 states: "The Church has an innate and proper right to coerce offending members of the Christian faithful by means of penal sanctions."

Penal sanctions are either medicinal or expiatory, depending on the offense. The term "medicinal" indicates the Church's desire for the offender to repent and be restored to the community. Excommunication is a medicinal penalty or censure. When a Catholic is excommunicated, that person is forbidden to participate in the Eucharist or in any sacramental celebrations of the Church. The excommunicated person is in danger of losing his eternal salvation.

Under present canon law, excommunication is attached to the following offenses against God and Church (this is only a partial list):

Apostasy, heresy, or schism; mistreatment of the elements of Holy Communion; physically attacking the pope; a priest absolving someone with whom he has committed sexual sin; pretending to be a priest and offering Mass and giving absolution in confession; ordaining a bishop without consent of the pope; any direct violation of the seal of confession; procuring an abortion.

Excommunication does not necessarily mean that a person will not be saved. However, the rebellion against the Church's teaching that brings about excommunication could indicate a deeper rebellion against God's authority.

I would like to call special attention to the last offense listed against God and Church. Canon 1398 reads: "A person who procures a completed abortion incurs an automatic excommunication." In view of this legislation, no Catholic should allow himself to become indifferent and calloused to the abortion-on-demand mentality prevailing in our modern world. In fact, anyone involved directly in the procedure to take the life of a preborn child is subject to this censure, including doctors, nurses, technicians, and so on.

This censure indicates the most serious condemnation and objection the Church has to this sin. The Church must uphold the tradition that a human person comes into existence at the moment of conception. That human person has the right, by divine law, to life, liberty, and the pursuit of happiness. May God grant that the civil laws of society come into conformity with God's law.

 How does one receive pardon from excommunication?

A Excommunication is removed by the fulfillment of two conditions: the repentance of the excommunicated individual and obtaining of pardon from one qualified to give it. Once an offender repents of the violation of Church order, the censure can be removed and the person restored to full communion with the Church. This may be done outside the sacrament of penance or within the sacrament, depending on the situation and the authority given the priest-confessor.

For example, in my diocese, every priest has the authority to reconcile completely and fully any woman who, while knowledgeable of the censure and the immorality of such an action, had an abortion, if she is now contrite and repentant. When a priest absolves a penitent from a censure outside the sacrament of penance, he says the following: "By the power granted to me, I absolve you from the bond of excommunication in the Name of the Father, and of the Son, and of the Holy Spirit."

This aspect of the "power of the keys of the kingdom" demonstrates the same mercy allowing the priest with apostolic authority to say: "I absolve you from your sins...." Praise be Jesus Christ for what his sacrifice on the cross makes possible. "All this has been done by God, who has reconciled us to himself through Christ and has given us the ministry of reconciliation" (2 Cor 5:18).

Q I believe God is speaking to his people through many different revelations, Marian and others. Why does the Catholic Church take so long to approve these kinds of messages?

A Many reported private revelations have proved erroneous, exaggerated, or even fraudulent, so the Church thoroughly investigates before giving approval, lest spiritual harm comes to those who believe in them. The Church takes seriously this duty to evaluate all such revelations in light of public revelation — all that God has revealed about himself, about us, and about his plan of salvation for us.

When the Church does approve a private revelation, it is saying that the revelation contains nothing contrary to faith and morals, that its message may be published, and that Catholics may believe the revelation, with caution. Authentic private revelations have clarified and deepened our understanding of existing truths, but they add no new doctrine to public revelation. Thus, Catholics are not obliged to believe the messages given through such revelations, because all that is necessary for our salvation has already been revealed to us through Scripture and Tradition.

As Pope John Paul II explained, "The Church has always taught and continues to proclaim that God's revelation was brought to completion in Jesus Christ, who is the fullness of that revelation, and that 'no new public revelation is to be expected before the glorious manifestation of the Lord' ("Dogmatic Constitution on the Church," No. 4). The Church evaluates and judges private revelations by the criterion of conformity with that single public revelation" (Address at Fatima, 1982).

Q I divorced my husband five years ago and now would like to find out if I can have my marriage annulled. What does it involve? Also, how much does it cost?

A An annulment is an official declaration of the Catholic Church that one or more of the conditions necessary for a valid, sacramental marriage were never met.

To begin the process, you should contact your diocesan tribunal, the ecclesiastical court of the Church. Usually, you'll be asked to fill out a questionnaire tracing the history of your courtship, marriage, and the breakdown of the relationship. Your answers will be reviewed to determine if grounds for annulment exist.

Some cases are fairly straightforward and involve a simple process: It could be easily proven if, for example, you had entered your marriage while still validly married to someone else. Other cases, such as those involving coercion, defective consent, fraud, or psychic incapacity to assume and fulfill the essential obligations of marriage, are more complex and require a more formal process.

If it is judged that grounds for annulment do exist and that the case can probably be proved, the other party is notified and given a chance to respond. Evidence is gathered, witnesses assembled, the case is heard by the tribunal, and the judges decide if the evidence for nullity is persuasive or not. All affirmative decisions for nullity are automatically reviewed by a higher court. If the decision is confirmed, the annulment is granted.

If the decision is negative, and the annulment is not granted, you have a couple of options. You can challenge the decision on procedural grounds or, even if the decision is procedurally correct, you may appeal it if you believe it to be unjust.

This process — and my description is greatly simplified — can take many months. The cost of an annulment differs from diocese to diocese and depends, to a certain degree, on the length of time involved. Money, however, is never an impediment to the annulment process. Even if you cannot afford the fees, your case will be heard if you have grounds for annulment. Approximately 60,000 annulments are granted every year in the United States.

Q My faith has been shaken by all the recent publicity about scandalous behavior among clergy. How should Catholics react to such news?

A No matter how shaken we are when someone in Church leadership is publicly accused of sin, we must remember that authentic Christianity cannot bypass the Church. Our personal relationship with Jesus Christ must remain solid, and that relationship still has to be supported by and shared with a eucharistic community presided over by an ordained presbyter or bishop. For this reason, daily prayer for bishops, priests, deacons, and religious is a necessary discipline of Catholic-Christian life. We should desire intensely that our ordained and vowed servants of the Church be persons proclaiming and living the full and authentic gospel of Jesus Christ.

Each and every baptized member of our Catholic Church should continue to "hunger and thirst for holiness" (Mt 5:6) regardless of the sins, alleged or real, of any clergyman or religious at any level of Church life. When a servant-leader falls from grace, our response is indeed sadness and pain and a profound concern for those offended. Along with this response should be a compassion for both the sinner and the sinned against. We should sincerely pray for both. We who follow Jesus must desire the repentance, rehabilitation, and restoration of the sinner. We must also be concerned about the healing and restoration to well-being of those sinned against or scandalized. The repentance of the servant-leader who falls is most urgent given the warning of Jesus that "scandals will inevitably arise, but woe to him through whom they come" (Lk 17:1).

I believe we can trust the leadership of our Catholic Church to care adequately for any failure or scandal that may arise from the inappropriate and sometimes reprehensible behavior of any vowed or ordained person in the Church. I also believe the vast majority of our clergy and religious are genuinely desirous of leading good and holy lives. And, though they don't get nearly the media coverage of those who have fallen, we can as a Church rejoice in the universally powerful witness of Pope John Paul II, Mother Teresa of Calcutta, and the countless other men and women of sanctity at every level of Church life. No matter what the negative publicity, maintain your love and loyalty for the Church of our Lord and Savior Jesus Christ, to whom he has given the promise: "the jaws of death shall not prevail against it" (Mt 16:18).

Q Is it true that Pope John Paul II has approved the use of altar girls? What's next — women priests?

A The Pope has confirmed that service at the altar can be performed by lay people, whether they are male or female.

This change was announced in a letter to bishops' conferences around the world dated mid-March and signed by Cardinal Antonio Javierre Ortas, prefect of the Congregation for Divine Worship and the Sacraments.

The letter states that the use of female altar servers is subject to the pastoral needs of local churches and is thus optional for each bishop; that altar boys represent a "noble tradition" that has led to priestly vocations and must continue to be supported; that any decision to use female altar servers should be explained well to the faithful; and that liturgical ministries exercised by lay people are temporary tasks subject to the bishop's judgment and do not imply a right held by either men or women.

I have no problem with this policy because I have always viewed service at the altar as simply another ministry such as reading the Scriptures or distributing Holy Communion, which have long been performed by women as well as men.

The answer to your second question is found in Pope John Paul II's apostolic letter, "On Reserving Priestly Ordination to Men Alone" (*Ordinatio Sacerdotalis*) issued on May 22, 1994. The Pope effectively closed the modern debate on women's ordination by stating, "Wherefore, in order that all doubt may be removed regarding a matter of great importance, a matter which pertains to the Church's divine constitution itself, in virtue of my ministry of confirming the brethren (cf. Lk 22:32) I declare that the Church has no authority whatsoever to confer priestly ordination on women and that this judgment is to be definitively held by all the Church's faithful" (No. 4).

The Pope traced the Church's teaching that priestly ordination is "reserved to men alone" from its scriptural and apostolic roots through the modern controversies surrounding the question of women's ordination. Quoting his Apostolic Letter *Mulieris Dignitatem*, he says, " 'In calling only men as his apostles, Christ acted in a completely free and sovereign manner. In doing so, he exercised the same freedom with which, in all his behavior, he emphasized the dignity and the vocation of women, without conforming to the prevailing customs and to the traditions sanctioned by the legislation of the time' " (No. 2).

He also says the fact that the Blessed Virgin Mary never received the ministerial priesthood shows that "the non-admission of women to priestly ordination cannot mean that women are of lesser dignity, nor can it be construed as discrimination against them. Rather, it is to be seen as the faithful observance of a plan to be ascribed to the wisdom of the Lord of the universe" (No. 3).

Calling the role of women in the life and mission of the Church "absolutely necessary and irreplaceable," the Pope recalled Paul VI's declaration, *Inter Insigniores*, which states, " 'The Church desires that Christian women should become fully aware of the greatness of their mission; today their role is of capital importance both for the renewal and humanization of society and for the rediscovery by believers of the true face of the Church' " (No. 3).

He concludes his discussion of the role of women in the Church with a reminder from *Inter Insigniores*, " 'The greatest in the kingdom of heaven are not the ministers but the saints' " (No. 3).

The Holy Father does not claim infallibility for this teaching, but "the letter does claim to give an infallible teaching," according to Father Augustine DiNoia, the top theologian in the U.S. Bishops' office in Washington.

"The best analogy is the Eucharist," Father DiNoia said. "You could argue, 'Why should we have bread and wine now? Bread and wine are not as important now as they were in the time of Jesus. Why should we continue to use them?'

"The only answer the Church can give is we know nothing of the Eucharist except as Christ gave it to us. So the elements are not optional. The same arguments are true of the priesthood. There would be no priesthood except that Christ instituted it. So we cannot alter or tamper with the fundamental structure that we have received."

This apostolic letter should calm the fears of those who thought the approval of women altar servers paved the way to women's ordination and remind all of us — male or female, priest or layperson — that our first role and highest calling is to "be made perfect as our heavenly father is perfect" (Mt 5:48).

Q Through being baptized in the Holy Spirit, my husband and I have grown in our appreciation for the Catholic Church. We feel led to express that appreciation in some form of service. Do you have any suggestions for ways lay people like us can serve the Church?

A Opportunities for lay service in the Catholic Church are increasing as the number of priests and religious is decreasing.

There are a variety of volunteer positions for Catholics in their local parishes, including lector, extraordinary minister of the Eucharist, religious education instructor, core leader of a prayer group, youth minister, and so on. Many parishes have outreaches to the poor that are in constant need of committed volunteers. The permanent diaconate (usually an unpaid position) is also an opportunity for a layman who feels called to serve in the Church in this important capacity.

Salaried positions on both the local and diocesan levels are also increasing. Some of these are coordinator of religious education, youth minister, pastoral assistant, elementary and high school teachers, and evangelism coordinator. Frankly, the salaried positions often involve financial sacrifice for a married man with a family, although the Church is beginning to realize that a family man will require a higher salary than our priests and religious.

You may find it necessary to return to school if you feel called to positions that require advanced degrees. The Master of Arts Program in Christian Ministry and Renewal offered by Franciscan University of Steubenville is an excellent way to prepare for active service in the Church.

My advice is that you and your husband pray for the Lord's direction in this area. Assess your talents, interests, and schedule, and speak to a local priest or layperson who is already involved in a Christian apostolate about opportunities in your diocese. I am confident that you will find an abundance of ways to put yourself at the service of the Lord.

Q When I introduced my brother-in-law to my parish priest, he kept using Father's first name when he addressed him. Later, I asked him why he didn't call him "Father," and he said the Bible tells us to call no man "father." Why do Catholics use the title "Father" when Jesus plainly said not to use it?

A Jesus uses a hyperbolic literary style to teach the important truth that God alone is our Father and Creator. If Matthew 23:9 was taken literally, as Christians we could not even call our biological fathers "father," let alone those who serve as our spiritual fathers.

The title "Father" has been used very naturally by Christians since apostolic times to refer to their spiritual fathers in the Lord. Jews and Christians alike considered the patriarchs Abraham, Isaac, Jacob, and others to be their "Fathers" in the faith (see Rom 4:16-17; 9:10).

St. Paul considered himself a spiritual father who compassionately and tenderly corrected his children: "I speak as a father to his children" (2 Cor 6:13). He admonished the Corinthians, saying, "Granted you have 10,000 guardians in

Christ, you have only one father. It was I who begot you in Christ Jesus through my preaching of the gospel" (1 Cor 4:15). St. John, in his first letter, appealed to Christians as his "children" (1 Jn 5:21).

In the first centuries of Christianity, holy men were often called "abbas" or "fathers," and the saints of the young Church (Ignatius of Antioch, Augustine, and Jerome, for example) later came to be known as the "fathers of the Church."

Does this ancient tradition of calling an ordained priest "Father" contradict Matthew 23:9, in which Jesus said, "Do not call anyone on earth your father. Only one is your father, the One in heaven"? No, it does not. That verse must be understood within the context of Matthew 23:1-12. In that passage, Jesus condemned the abuse of authority by those who selfishly seek after honor and social status instead of acknowledging that all authority comes from God our Father and is to be used to serve him and one another with humility and love.

Q My daughter married outside of the Catholic Church, and for many years she has attended her husband's church. Now she is wondering if she can be received back into the Catholic Church. She thinks she was excommunicated when she got married in her husband's church. Is she right?

A At one time, those who married outside of the Catholic Church were excommunicated. However, the law of the Church in this critical area has changed. Your daughter is not considered excommunicated, but she may not receive the sacraments until she has been officially reconciled with the Church.

The process of reconciliation for your daughter involves having her marriage validated or approved by the Church. She should contact a priest in her area or call the chancery office of her diocese for details about how to proceed.

Q I was at a couple of Masses where the Our Father was said in Latin. I like to pray the Mass in the vernacular so I can understand what I am saying. Could you explain all the interest in returning to Latin in the Mass?

A I too love to celebrate the Mass in my own language and am glad that restrictions on the use of the vernacular were gradually lifted in the years following Vatican II.

Some people believe that the use of Latin is more reverent than the use of the vernacular. Others are overly nostalgic about the use of Latin in the Mass. I agree that we should respect our traditions and the fact that Latin is still considered a revered language of the Catholic Church. However, I think we can fail to appreciate what the Holy Spirit is doing in the Church in the present if we cling too much to the past.

Learning some prayers and songs in Latin might be a good way of respecting our heritage and being sensitive to those who miss the Latin liturgy. Where appropriate and on occasion I would favor a Latin liturgy accompanied by adequate catechesis.

Q Today there seems to be much dissent within the Church, with even clergy and religious openly expressing disagreement with the Pope and ignoring instructions from Rome. What is your attitude toward this trend?

A With so many opinions about Catholic truth being circulated today, confusion and disagreement abounds, creating ideal conditions for Satan to foster disunity and loss of solidarity in our Catholic faith. To counteract this trend, we need to take seriously the discipline of the Church expressed in the new *Code of Canon Law*. "The Christian faithful, conscious of their own responsibility, are bound by Christian obedience to follow what the sacred pastors, as representatives of Christ, declare as teachers of the faith or determine as leaders of the Church" (Canon 212).

We need to obediently follow those disciplines that are for the common good and give obedience to the truth taught by our "sacred pastors" (bishops, including the Pope). Various degrees of assent are specified in Canons 750-754. I list four of them here for your meditation and reflection, and urge you to read them under the anointing of the Holy Spirit:

"All that is contained in the written word of God or in Tradition, that is, in the one deposit of faith entrusted to the Church and also proposed as divinely revealed either by the solemn Magisterium of the Church or by its ordinary and universal Magisterium, must be believed with divine and catholic faith; it is manifested by the common adherence of the Christian faithful under the leadership of the sacred Magisterium; therefore, all are bound to avoid any doctrines whatever which are contrary to these truths" (Canon 750).

"A religious respect of intellect and will, even if not the assent of faith, is to be paid to the teaching which the Supreme Pontiff or the college of bishops enunciate on faith or morals when they exercise the authentic Magisterium even if they do not intend to proclaim it with a definitive act; therefore the Christian faithful are to take care to avoid whatever is not in harmony with that teaching" (Canon 752).

"Although they do not enjoy infallible teaching authority, the bishops in communion with the head and members of the college, whether as individuals or gathered in conferences of bishops or in particular councils, are authentic teachers and instructors of the faith for the faithful entrusted to their care; the faithful must adhere to the authentic teaching of their own bishops with a religious assent of soul" (Canon 753).

"All the Christian faithful are obliged to observe the constitutions and decrees which the legitimate authority of the Church issues in order to propose doctrine and proscribe erroneous opinions; this is especially true of the constitutions and decrees issued by the Roman Pontiff or the college of bishops" (Canon 754).

One final suggestion. The new *Catechism of the Catholic Church* (*Libreria Editrice Vaticana*) was released in English in 1994. You should purchase one from your local Catholic bookstore and begin to read, study, and reflect on its contents. This will be one of the best ways you can form your conscience, grow in comprehension of authentic Catholic Christian teaching, experience renewal of your mind, and be equipped for further growth in holiness. Alongside the Sacred Scriptures, the *Catechism* should become your most-used source of information and wisdom about what God wants you to know for a more abundant life here and hereafter.

May assent to the truth of God revealing himself and his will, rather than dissent, become the norm in our holy Catholic Church.

Q Many years ago I left the Catholic Church because of a painful experience in my parish. Now I am reconsidering that decision. What should I do to return?

A First, I'd like to ask your forgiveness on behalf of anyone who ever hurt you or ignored your needs in the Church. The Church is made up of human beings, sinners and saints, who are often not as loving and understanding as the Lord calls us to be with one another.

You have a special home in the Catholic Church, and the door is always open for you. Find a priest in your area with whom you can share your story (perhaps a friend could make a recommendation if you do not know one). He may be able to help you work through the experience that made you leave and direct you to a group or class for inactive Catholics that could smooth your way back into the Church.

My heartfelt hope and prayer is that you will be reconciled with the Church and return to active life in it. Celebrating the sacrament of penance with an understanding priest will bring you into full communion with the Church once more.

Q It's clear from Scripture that priests and bishops were allowed to be married in the early Church. Why did the Catholic Church change the rules so priests are now required to be celibate?

A The clearest explanation I've come across is in the Second Vatican Council's "Decree on the Ministry and Life of Priests," (*Presbyterorum Ordinis*). It says:

"Perfect and perpetual continence for the sake of the kingdom of heaven was recommended by Christ the Lord. It has been freely accepted and laudably observed by many Christians down through the centuries as well as in our own time, and has always been highly esteemed in a special way by the Church as a feature of priestly life.... It is true that it is not demanded of the priesthood by its nature.

"There are many ways in which celibacy is in harmony with the priesthood.... By preserving virginity or celibacy for the sake of the kingdom of heaven priests are consecrated in a new and excellent way to Christ. They more readily cling to him with undivided heart and dedicate themselves more freely in him and through him to the service of God and of men. They are less encumbered in their service of his kingdom and of the task of heavenly regeneration. In this way they become better fitted for a broader acceptance of fatherhood in Christ.

"By means of celibacy, then, priests profess before men their willingness to be dedicated with undivided loyalty to the task entrusted to them, namely that of espousing the faithful to one husband and presenting them as a chaste virgin to Christ. They recall that mystical marriage, established by God and destined to be fully revealed in the future, by which the Church holds Christ as her only spouse. Moreover they are made a living sign of that world to come, already present through faith and charity, a world in which the children of the Resurrection shall neither be married nor take wives.

"For these reasons, based on the mystery of Christ and his mission, celibacy, which at first was recommended to priests, was afterwards in the Latin Church imposed by law on all who were to be promoted to Holy Orders" (No. 16).

Even though the Roman Catholic Church holds fast to celibacy as an important part of the call to priesthood, this is a discipline that could be changed by the Church, if the bishops and pope were led by the Spirit to do this. We must also acknowledge those married men (most notably those who have left the Episcopal Church) who have been ordained priests and are now serving in various ways within the Catholic Church. In fact, the universal Church in union with Rome has both celibate and married priests actively ministering, though the more common clerical discipline remains celibacy.

Q Why does the canonization process take so long?

A In his book, *Making Saints* (Simon and Schuster), Kenneth L. Woodward details the history of the canonization process and the changes initiated in it by Pope John Paul II. Though I believe he overemphasizes the politics of the process, I don't know of any clearer, recent explanation of canonization.

In the past, the canonization process put the life, writings, and death of the servant of God (the candidate for sainthood) on trial. Just as in secular trials, this involved a great amount of time, work, and expense. The process has now shifted from the courtroom model to the academic model of researching and writing a doctoral dissertation, but the Catholic Church still proceeds cautiously before declaring anyone a model of heroic Christian virtue.

Even if the cause moves forward quickly it can be many years between its introduction and the pope's act of canonization declaring that the person now reigns in eternal glory and decreeing that the Church show him the honor due to a saint. When the process hits a snag, there's no telling how long it may take.

Sometimes a cause is held up because of concerns about the orthodoxy of the servant of God's writings. Sometimes the Church recognizes his sanctity, but the requisite number of miracles (two for non-martyrs) attributed to his intercession are not forthcoming. Money is another problem. If the group working to advance the cause can no longer fund the process, the cause is set aside — sometimes permanently, sometimes until the necessary funds are raised to reinstate it.

Q I know the Third Commandment is "Remember to keep holy the Lord's day," but I often wonder what it means to keep it holy.

A The Catholic Church defines this commandment as follows: "On Sundays and other holy days of obligation the faithful are bound to participate in the Mass; they are also to abstain from those labors and business concerns which impede the worship to be rendered to God, the joy which is proper to the Lord's day, or the proper relaxation of mind and body" (Canon 1247).

Consult your confessor or spiritual director if you have difficulty in applying this principle.

Chapter IV: Prayer and Worship

Q I'm getting discouraged about my parish church's dull liturgies. They just do not offer the Spirit-filled, vibrant, joyful worship that I need to grow in my relationship with the Lord. Is there anything a person in my situation can do, short of leaving the Catholic Church?

A I understand how hungry you are to experience the power of the Holy Spirit and to be nourished spiritually by the Scriptures in your local church community, but I would not advise you to leave the Catholic Church, which is your spiritual home.

Ask the Lord to speak to you about how your spiritual needs can be satisfied in the Catholic Church. Perhaps another Catholic parish in your area would be more spiritually nourishing for you, and you should consider joining it if the Lord leads you to do so.

You also need to remember that although the worship at your Sunday liturgy is not as "charismatic" in style as you might hope, you are still coming into a very intimate time of communication with the Lord when you receive his body and blood during Holy Communion.

One of my tapes that might help you get more out of the Mass is "The Sacramental Life: Keys to Parish Renewal" (Servant). Some books that you might read are: *And Their Eyes Were Opened: Encountering Jesus in the Sacraments* (Servant) by

Father Michael Scanlan, T.O.R. and Ann Shields; *The Bible and the Mass* (Servant) by Father Peter Stravinskas; and Chapter 3 of *The Catholic Challenge* (Servant) by Alan Schreck.

Finally, I encourage you to hope in the Lord and to intercede for a greater outpouring of the Holy Spirit on the Catholic Church and upon all Christian churches. The Catholic Church needs strongly committed Christians like you who love Jesus with all their hearts to be a light of his love to others and to help bring about the spiritual renewal that we as individuals and as Church need so desperately.

Q I have been wondering what it means when we pray "thy kingdom come." Are we asking for heaven?

A In Matthew 6:9-13 and in Luke 11:2-4 we are taught to pray for the coming of the "kingdom" or "reign" of God. Jesus gave the kingdom of God first place in his preaching. He announced the good news that with his coming "This is the time of fulfillment. The reign of God is at hand!" (Mk 1:15).

The miracles Jesus performed are signs of the kingdom's presence. With his coming, the domination of Satan, of sin, and of death over humanity is at an end. By raising Jesus from the dead, God has conquered death, and in the person of Jesus, God has definitively established his kingdom. "Therefore let the whole house of Israel know beyond any doubt that God has made both Lord and Messiah this Jesus whom you crucified" (Acts 2:36; see also Mt 28:18).

To enter this kingdom we must submit to the King, who is Jesus the Christ. The person of the King and the reality of the kingdom are one. To enter the kingdom we must believe in Jesus and be baptized in water and Spirit. "I solemnly assure you, no one can enter into God's kingdom without being begotten of water and Spirit" (Jn 3:5). Jesus, through the post-Pentecost community of his Church, calls each person to be converted, to make a radical decision to follow him and his teachings so as to allow God to "reign" or "rule" over his or her life. Under this rule, our interior and exterior lives will be changed for the better by the dynamic activity of the Holy Spirit (see Acts 2:38).

Thus when we pray "thy kingdom come" we are really praying for the Holy Spirit to come upon us and transform us. We are likewise praying as disciples of Christ who "recognize that the kingdom is already present in the person of Jesus and is slowly being established within humanity and the world through a mysterious connection with him" (*Redemptoris Missio*, No. 16). We are praying for all to be converted to Christ; for all to be baptized with the Holy Spirit; for all to be obedient to the will of God here and now ("… thy will be done on earth as it is in heaven"). We are praying for all to become members of the Church; we are praying for all to be saved (see Acts 2:47). John Paul II reminds us that "the kingdom cannot be detached either from Christ or from the Church" (*Redemptoris Missio*, No. 18). Any comprehension of the "kingdom of God" that ignores either Christ or the Church is not biblical.

Our prayer is both for a reality yet to come in its plenitude and for an outpouring of the Holy Spirit that will convert people's hearts and minds as we submit to the King. We express our yearning for the day when Christ our King will present to the Father "an eternal and universal kingdom: a kingdom of truth and life, a kingdom of holiness and grace, a kingdom of justice, love, and peace" ("Preface to the Mass of Christ the King").

Obviously there are successive phases of this mysterious reality called "kingdom." The kingdom is already here among us in the presence of Christ, and it always will be present in the activity of the Holy Spirit: "Know that I am with you always, until the end of the world!" (Mt 28:20).

But the parables of growth (the seed, the mustard seed, the

leaven, the tares and good wheat, the fish in Matthew 13) tell us there is a time of unfolding between the historical inauguration of the kingdom and its full realization at the end of this age. We presently live in the time of the Church, the time of witness: "You will receive power when the Holy Spirit comes down on you; then you are to be my witnesses … to the ends of the earth" (Acts 1:8). Our prayer is very much for the present, with a longing for the future, when the King and the kingdom will arrive in all fullness and majesty (see Rev 21:4).

When we pray the Lord's Prayer we are serving the kingdom, which is God's gift and work. "We must ask for the kingdom, welcome it, and make it grow within us; but we must also work together so that it will be welcomed and will grow among all people, until the time when Christ 'delivers the kingdom to God the Father' and 'God will be everything to everyone' (1 Cor 15:24,28)" (*Redemptoris Missio*, No. 20).

I have only dwelt on a few dimensions of one verse of this prayer. How magnificent, awesome, and powerful is the entire prayer Jesus teaches his disciples to say. May we really mean it wholeheartedly when we pray each and every day: "Thy kingdom come."

Q I have been told that perpetual adoration of the Eucharist is not a "liturgically sound" devotion. Please tell me about the regulations governing perpetual adoration as I would like to get this started in our parish.

A The present liturgical norms that govern exposition of the Blessed Sacrament distinguish three kinds of exposition: that for a lengthy period, that for a brief period, and perpetual eucharistic adoration or adoration over extended periods of time practiced by some religious communities and other groups.

All of these forms of worship of the Holy Eucharist outside of Mass are highly recommended, provided they avoid "anything which might somehow obscure the principal desire of Christ in instituting the Eucharist to be with us as food, medicine, and comfort" (*The Rites of the Catholic Church*, Pueblo Publishing, 1976, "Holy Communion and Worship of the Eucharist Outside Mass," No. 82). Thus there must always be manifested a relationship between eucharistic worship outside of Mass and the eucharistic celebration of Mass itself. Perhaps in their zeal to give primary place to the celebration of the sacrifice of the Mass, some have understated and even ignored the clear teachings of the Church "that all the faithful show this holy sacrament the veneration and adoration which is due to God himself, as has always been customary in the Catholic Church. Nor is the sacrament to be less the object of adoration because it was instituted by Christ the Lord to be received as food" ("Holy Communion," No. 3).

I give thanks to God that there is a revival in eucharistic devotion, no doubt due to the example of Pope John Paul II himself, who has established exposition of the Blessed Sacrament in St. Peter's Basilica when that church is open. Any form of perpetual adoration in a parish church or other diocesan setting would, of course, have to be instituted with the permission of the local bishop. Other forms of exposition are at the discretion of the local clergy who must observe the revised rituals governing such celebrations.

The reforms of the Second Vatican Council make it clear that we are indeed to be a people of the Word and the Sacrament.

Q I moved to a new city last fall and have finally found a parish where I really feel welcome. The problem is that I don't live within the territory of the parish I want to join. Am I permitted to register there, or must I register at the parish within whose boundaries I reside?

A Canon law says that bishops should organize parishes on a geographic basis, but that personal (non-territorial) parishes are also possible. These can be "based upon rite, language, the nationality of the Christian faithful within some territory, or even upon some other determining factor" (Canon 518).

Similarly, the Catholic faithful may take factors other than geography into account when deciding on a parish. Canon law says that the parish should be seen as a *community* of the Christian faithful. Many bishops, recognizing that not everyone experiences a sense of community within the territorial parish, allow Catholics to register across traditional geographic parish boundaries.

The rules in this regard vary from diocese to diocese. To find out how your bishop approaches this question, ask the priest in the parish you wish to join or call the diocesan office.

Q I've been reading a daily Scripture study guide put out by a Protestant organization, but recently I've started looking for a Catholic guide. Can you recommend one?

A *God's Word Today*, which is edited by *New Covenant*'s "Your Word" columnist George Martin, is a daily guide to reading Scripture that focuses on a different biblical personality, topic, or book of the Bible each month. For subscription information write to *God's Word Today*, 5615 W. Cermak Road, Cicero, Illinois 60650-2290, or call: (708) 656-8259.

The Word Among Us is a Scripture study guide and commentary that follows the daily Mass readings. It is published by Mother of God Community in Maryland. For subscription information call 1-800-638-8539.

Another resource is the Catholic Study Bible published by Oxford University Press. It has become my constant companion.

I highly recommend all of these publications and strongly encourage Christians to spend time reading and studying Scripture every day.

Q I noticed that some days on my parish calendar are marked as memorials, some as optional memorials, some as feasts, and some as solemnities. What's the difference?

A Being a Catholic Christian is a way of life. As members of the Church, we celebrate the saving work of Jesus throughout the year, using a specially designed liturgical year and calendar with accompanying liturgical texts, Scriptures, and prayers.

Each week on Sunday, the Lord's Day, we commemorate the Resurrection of Jesus Christ, the head of the Church. Once a year at Easter we celebrate his Resurrection and Passion with the utmost solemnity. Throughout the yearly cycle of our Church calendar, we observe the entire mystery of Christ and the anniversaries of the saints.

Each day of the year is made holy by our celebration of Mass and praying the Liturgy of the Hours (the Divine Office). The liturgical day runs from midnight to midnight, except for Sundays and solemnities, which begin at sundown the evening before. For this reason we can celebrate Sunday Mass on Saturday evening. Our Jewish heritage is clearly demonstrated in this custom.

Sunday is ranked as the first holy day of all. Its observance by Catholics is a most serious obligation.

According to their importance, liturgical celebrations and observances are distinguished from each other. They are solemnities, feasts, and memorials. The two greatest solemnities are Easter and Christmas. Their observance goes on for eight days.

Feasts are next in rank, followed by memorials, which are either obligatory or optional. The days following Sunday are called weekdays, and they are celebrated in different ways according to the importance each one has.

The liturgical year and calendar are major instruments for the formation of Christ's faithful "by means of devotional practices, both interior and exterior, instruction, and works of penance and mercy" ("General Norms for the Liturgical Year and the Calendar," No. 1). When you become accustomed to following the liturgical calendar as a way of life, I can assure you from personal experience that your prayer life takes on more meaning and variety. Your emotions and moods are even affected positively, and your reflective thinking for the day disciples you into a deeper relationship with the living Christ, whose reality is so infinite that we need to take weeks and seasons to gradually understand and live out the awesome truth of what he has done and is doing to save us.

Being inspired by the lives of the saints, and especially the life of Mary, our Mother, and walking with Christ, our Savior, through his life, Death, Resurrection, Ascension, and sending of the Spirit, further edifies and builds us up into a people who are truly "light to the world and salt to the earth" (see Mt 5:13-14). Liturgical spirituality is the way we are formed as a people of God. It is the primary school of discipleship. It is the primary formation program for becoming adult and committed Catholics.

For further study, I refer you to the official liturgical publications of the United States Catholic Conference Publishing Services in Washington, D.C., telephone 1-800-235-USCC.

Q Our pastor put a notice in our bulletin asking parents to take their children to the cry room during Mass if the children scream or are otherwise disruptive. Many parents complained about the notice and refuse to follow the pastor's instructions. What do you do about screaming children at Mass?

A I preach louder!
Though I can usually make myself heard, I agree that children who are agitated should be taken from the assembly either into a cry room or into another room where they will not

distract others. Parents should do this out of respect for the rest of the worshiping community. I believe the pastor was perfectly correct in attempting to educate the people of his parish in the appropriate steps to take in this situation. I understand why some may be upset, but that should not stop them from trying to correct the situation.

Q I've been wanting to do some spiritual reading in addition to reading the Bible, but there are so many books I don't know where to start. Do you have any recommendations for me?

A Of the spiritual classics, I recommend St. Francis de Sales' devotional masterpiece, *Introduction to the Devout Life*, and *The Confessions of St. Augustine*, both of which are available in beautiful modern translations.

I also recommend the classic, *Practicing the Presence of God*, by Brother Lawrence, which is available in any good bookstore. Many spiritual classics, including *The Imitation of Christ*, are available in paperback from Image Books, an imprint of Doubleday Press in New York City. A catalog worth sending for is that of St. Paul Books and Media in Boston (1-800-876-4463). They also have information on the publications of Father Benedict Groeschel, C.F.R., whose writings and tapes will truly inspire and edify you.

Alphonsus Liguori: The Redeeming Love of Christ (New City Press), a collection of the saint's spiritual writings edited by Joseph Oppitz, C.S.S.R., also gives the reader much food for reflection and meditation.

Many of Capuchin Father Raniero Cantalamessa's books have recently been translated from Italian into English, including *Life in the Lordship of Christ* (Sheed & Ward) and *Jesus Christ: The Holy One of God* (Liturgical Press). Father Cantalamessa serves as preacher to the papal household, giving weekly homilies to the Holy Father during Lent and Advent.

Finally, I have just purchased and am enjoying the seven-volume series titled *Conversation with God* (Scepter Press) by Father Francis Fernandez. He presents inspiring meditations and reflections of depth following the Church's liturgical readings for each day of the year. This series is available from Leaflet Missal Company of St. Paul, Minnesota (1-800-328-9582).

You can find out about good spiritual reading in publishers' catalogs, such as Our Sunday Visitor (1-800-348-2440), Liguori (1-800-325-9521), Servant ((313) 761-8505), and others. Your local public library can help you find additional books and publishers' addresses, free of charge.

May the Lord, through his Holy Spirit, guide you in your spiritual reading along with your daily reflection upon Sacred Scripture.

Q I don't think we need the Rosary, the Way of the Cross, novenas, and so on, because we have the Mass. Why does the Catholic Church allow so many different devotions?

A You are right in believing that the Mass is far superior to any popular religious devotion. As Vatican II teaches, "Every liturgical celebration, because it is an action of Christ the Priest and of his body, which is the Church, is a sacred action surpassing all others. No other action of the Church can equal its efficacy by the same title and to the same degree" ("Constitution on the Sacred Liturgy," No. 7).

The Council Fathers also acknowledged that "the spiritual life, however, is not limited solely to participation in the liturgy" ("Sacred Liturgy," No. 12) and further stated, "Popular devotions of the Christian people, provided they conform to the laws and norms of the Church, are to be highly recommended" ("Sacred Liturgy," No. 13).

Many popular devotions arose in response to a particular need in the Church at a specific time in history. St. Dominic is believed to have spread devotion to the Rosary in the Middle Ages as an antidote to the Albigensian heresy, which maintained that all matter was intrinsically evil, and denied the Incarnation. The Way of the Cross evolved from a strong devotion to the Passion and Death of Jesus Christ in the twelfth and thirteenth centuries. Now prayed especially during the liturgical season of Lent, the Way of the Cross still leads us to meditate deeply on Christ's sacrifice for us.

I also believe it is no coincidence that the Chaplet of Divine Mercy is becoming so popular in this century, when there is so much evidence of the widespread indifference of the world to the Lord Jesus Christ. By beatifying Sister Faustina Kowalska, who received the revelations of Divine Mercy, Pope John Paul II seems to be approving this as a special devotion for our time.

As long as devotions "harmonize with the liturgical seasons, accord with the sacred liturgy, are in some way derived from it, and lead the people to it" ("Sacred Liturgy," No. 13), they may be embraced wholeheartedly as a means of encouraging spiritual growth and communion with God.

Q You are an evangelist and a diocesan priest. What form does your personal spirituality take? Maybe sharing such a personal note will encourage many of us who also have a very active life.

A The entire fourth chapter of Paul's Second Letter to the Corinthians is my very special passage in Sacred Scripture and influences my daily life of service to the Lord. Verse 5 provides my personal motto: "It is not ourselves we preach but Christ Jesus as Lord, and ourselves as your servants for Jesus' sake."

To sustain myself in this posture of a servant-preacher, my spirituality is primarily liturgical and ecclesial. By that I mean that the primary form of my prayer life is the Liturgy of the Hours. The primary sources of my daily meditations are the assigned liturgical readings for each day as found in the official *Lectionary of the Church.* Within this structure I also make use of spontaneous praise and intercession as well as the gift of tongues.

I usually celebrate Morning Prayer and the Office of Readings before the presence of the Lord in the Blessed Sacrament. My custom is to spend one hour of uninterrupted prayer and meditation in that setting. I pause for the Daytime Hours of Midmorning, Midday, and Midafternoon Prayer at my desk or wherever I may find myself ministering. For Midafternoon Prayer I usually add the Chaplet of Divine Mercy, which I have come to find as a consoling and powerful form of prayer. Following Evening Prayer I add the Rosary. The day always ends with Night Prayer offered just before bedtime.

Throughout the day I seek moments to nourish myself with one chapter from the Old and New Testaments and at least three paragraphs from the Vatican II documents, which I began to reread this past year.

In addition to this disciplined prayer, I very much believe the Holy Spirit helps me develop a sense of God's presence all through the day and evening. He is everywhere, and " 'in him we live and move and have our being' " (Acts 17:28). Using traditional aspirations at any time of day or night can assist in such an awareness. My favorite is "Jesus, I trust in you." Even if I am busy about many things I can maintain a certain reverence toward the Lord at strategic times by using my alarm watch. With discipline, it is possible to regulate one's schedule to give due time to direct worship of God. I have learned not to be a slave of the phone or doorbell. Using answering devices I can control the traffic and guard that precious time with the Lord. Rarely is a call or a visit an emergency.

Following the prompting of the Holy Spirit is very important in all of this. When I do not feel like praying I just ask the Lord to send the wave of desire that is the breath of his divine

Presence. Now more than ever I know why our liturgical tradition has us start every hour of prayer with: "God, come to my assistance. Lord, make haste to help me." We cannot even pray without God's help. All is grace; all is mercy.

At the center of my day, of course, is the celebration of Holy Mass. It is at the Table of the Lord that I am most priest. It is from the Table that I am primarily nourished by the living presence of the Crucified and Risen One. It is to the Table I bring all of the prayer intentions that come my way from parish ministry and evangelistic outreach. It is in Communion with my eucharistic community that the highest form of praise and thanksgiving is offered each day.

I hope my personal sharing will be of help to you. May I conclude by underlining the attitude that has to undergird every spirituality: The Christian life is a life of ongoing conversion. I have a profound awareness that I am basically weak and quite capable of sin. Relying on Christ as Savior and Lord of all must be the foundation of one's personal walk and spirituality. A spirituality that does not center on the crucified and risen Christ is not part of our Tradition. I also believe we must "pray and think with the Church." Thus my personal piety takes a secondary place to the liturgical prayer life of the Church; liturgy provides the framework and a way of living. Within that framework one can add and benefit from many other devotions and forms of piety.

Q What version of the Bible do you recommend for Catholics?

A Catholic Bibles include seven Old Testament books that are not found in the King James Version or in many other Protestant versions. The Catholic Church holds these books to be canonical and inspired, while Protestants do not. Sometimes the seven books can be found in Protestant versions as "Apocryphal" or "Deuterocanonical" books. The New

Testaments of both Catholic and Protestant Bibles have the same twenty-seven books.

I use the New American Bible (NAB) for preaching and teaching purposes. It is also the version presently used liturgically in most Catholic churches in this country. The NAB contains introductory articles and insightful notes and cross references to assist readers in understanding the Scriptures. You can find it at your local Catholic bookstore.

For study purposes I also use the New Jerusalem Bible (NJB) and the New International Version (NIV). Also, I recently purchased the Catholic Study Bible published by Oxford University Press.

Chapter V: Doctrine

Q About once a month, I like to attend a charismatic nondenominational church instead of going to Mass on Sunday. Sometimes I don't go to either church. My wife says that I must attend Mass every Sunday, even if I go to the nondenominational church. What does the Catholic Church teach about Mass attendance?

A Although it can be a good thing to attend another Christian service occasionally, your wife is correct. Canon 1247 of the *Code of Canon Law* states that on Sundays and other holy days of obligation, the faithful are bound to participate in the Mass.

The Catholic Church has always affirmed the scriptural importance of honoring the Lord's day in light of the third commandment, "Remember to keep holy the sabbath day." That includes attending the communal celebration of the Lord's Supper on the Lord's day: "We should not absent ourselves from the assembly, as some do, but encourage one another; and this all the more because you see that the day draws near" (Heb 10:25; see also Ps 50:5). Many other Scriptures give evidence that the first Christian communities assembled on the Lord's day or Sunday (see Rev 1:10) to honor and worship the Lord and celebrate the Eucharist (see 1 Cor 11:17-34; Acts 2:42).

The Christian life is a communal life, and we should hold it as a joy and a very serious obligation to worship our Lord with our brothers and sisters on the day he has set aside as holy. Since the Church considers it a sign of our love and commitment to the Lord to attend Mass on Sunday with our Church family, it is a serious matter to choose not to attend Sunday Mass if you are healthy and able to attend.

Q My precious three-year-old son almost died in an auto accident six months ago. Because I am a nonpracticing Catholic, I've never had him baptized. Now I wonder if he would have gone to limbo if he'd died. What do you think?

A Although it is often taught as a common solution to such a question, the existence of limbo has never been officially endorsed by the Church as a certain and defined doctrine.

Scripture teaches us that all human beings suffer the consequences of original sin, which alienates us from God, and that all of us need the salvation that comes only from Jesus Christ. Because of this, the Catholic Church has always taught that it is important for a child's salvation that he or she is baptized.

The idea of limbo was put forward by theologians in the Church as one possible explanation of the eternal destiny of infants and children who die unbaptized. It was described as a state of peace and happiness in which they experience neither suffering nor the full joys of heaven.

Today some theologians believe that God in his mercy allows even unbaptized children to enter into the fullness of life with him in heaven. I am inclined to agree with these theologians. However, because baptism is ordinarily necessary for salvation, Canon 867 of Church law states, "Parents are obliged to see to it that infants are baptized within the first weeks after birth." The Church is also very concerned about the pastoral preparation of the parents prior to the celebration of baptism.

Q The Catholic Church teaches that it is the one, true church, yet it does not give the same assurance of salvation that other churches do. Why can't I confidently say, "once saved, always saved," like some of my evangelical friends do?

A The Catholic Church's teaching does differ from that of some evangelical Christians in this area. "Once saved, always saved" is a slogan by which some evangelicals summarize their belief that once you've repented of your sin and accepted Jesus Christ as your Lord and Savior, you are saved for all eternity. The Catholic understanding of our assurance of salvation is a confident hope or inner assurance of the heart rather than an absolute certainty. The Church holds that you could lose the hope of salvation if you completely reject Jesus Christ after coming into a relationship with him.

Although the Lord has forgiven all of our sins by his sacrifice upon the cross (see 1 Jn 1:7), it is still possible for us to reject him and suffer the consequences of our sins. As St. Paul says, "Let anyone who thinks he is standing upright watch out lest he fall!" (1 Cor 10:12).

God gives us a confident hope of salvation when we are living in a close relationship with him. But, he also calls us to run the race to completion and to hunger and thirst for holiness if we are to receive the salvation for which we hope. Jesus said in Matthew 24:13, "The man who holds out to the end, however, is the one who will see salvation."

Our commitment to Jesus needs to be a daily commitment of our hearts to him and not just a onetime prayer of acceptance that is not accompanied by a life of holiness characterized by the fruit of the Holy Spirit.

Q I am concerned that many Catholics don't believe in purgatory. Aren't we required to believe this doctrine? Would you please explain purgatory using Scripture references?

A The *1991 Catholic Almanac* (Our Sunday Visitor) defines purgatory this way: "The state or condition in which those who have died in the state of grace, but with some attachment to sin, suffer for a time before they are admitted to the glory and happiness of heaven. In this state and period of passive suffering, they are purified of unrepented venial sins, satisfy the demands of divine justice for temporal punishment due for sins, and are thus converted to a state of worthiness of the beatific vision."

As a doctrine of the Church, all Catholics must believe in the existence of purgatory. The word "purgatory" is not found in the Bible, but its existence is implied in many biblical texts and in the ancient Tradition of the Church.

The Old Testament passage most commonly cited in support of the doctrine of purgatory is 2 Maccabees 12:39-45, in which Judas Maccabee's army prayed for those who died in battle and took up a collection to have sacrifices offered that the dead might be freed of their sin. The author of Maccabees comments, "If he [Judas Maccabee] were not expecting the fallen to rise again, it would have been useless and foolish to pray for them in death.... Thus he made atonement for the dead that they might be freed from this sin" (2 Mc 12:44, 46).

Certain New Testament texts (see Mt 12:32; 2 Tim 1:18; 1 Cor 3:10-15) also imply the existence of purgatory, but the greatest evidence for this doctrine is found in Christian Tradition. The early Church never accepted the belief that the soul of every person who dies in the state of grace goes immediately to heaven, and it was a common practice to pray and offer good deeds for the dead.

As Dr. Alan Schreck points out in his book, *Catholic and Christian* (Servant), "Praying for the dead makes sense only if those prayers can benefit the dead. If they had already arrived at their final eternal destiny, heaven or hell, then praying for the dead would be futile. However, if the deceased were undergoing the healing and purification of purgatory, then prayer for God's mercy on them would be reasonable and fitting."

Catholics see purgatory as one more sign of God's love and mercy. Because God is all holy and nothing unclean or sinful can stand before him, he would be justified in condemning even those who had lived good lives if they died unrepentant for venial sins. Instead, in his mercy, he provides for the purification of these souls, so that they may be able to see him face to face.

Q What happens to the poor souls in purgatory who have no one to pray for them? I was told as a child that they were lost, never to see God's face. Is that true?

A No. The souls in purgatory are already saved, but they are undergoing a period of purification that will enable them to see God face-to-face.

The Catholic Church prays for all those in purgatory at every Mass. In Canon II, for example, the priest says, "Remember our brothers and sisters who have gone to their rest in the hope of rising again. Bring them and all the departed into the light of your presence." And, of course, on All Souls' Day, November 2, the Church especially remembers and prays for the souls in purgatory.

Q My wife, who is a fundamentalist, heard Mary called "Mediatrix of All Graces." She understands this to mean that all grace flows through Mary, and without Mary there is no grace. Since Mary, however special she is, is human and not God, how can this be?

A In the Vatican II document, *Dogmatic Constitution on the Church*, we find the answer to your main question. It states that Mary is invoked in the Church under the title of Mediatrix, but that this title is understood in a way that "neither takes away anything from nor adds anything to the dignity and efficacy of Christ the one Mediator" (No. 62).

Christ's mediation is indeed unique, the document explains, but not exclusive. Thus, Mary is able to share in his mediation although she remains a human creature subordinate to Jesus Christ.

The Catholic Church teaches that Mary has this prominent role as Mediatrix because God chose her to be intimately involved in his plan of redemption. All grace flows through Mary, because it was through her "Yes" to God that Jesus, the source of all graces, came into the world.

The Church does *not* teach, as your wife believes, that there is no grace without Mary. Jesus Christ acquired the graces necessary for redemption through his Passion, Death, and Resurrection. He is the source of all graces; Mary is the channel through which they come to us.

Some theologians believe that we receive no grace without Mary's intercession. This does not mean that we must always ask for God's grace in Mary's name, but that we receive grace through her intercession whether we use her name or not. (The Church holds this as a legitimate opinion, not as a point of doctrine.)

The Church in no way means to hinder our relationship to Jesus by teaching us about Mary. Rather, it hopes that we will be encouraged by her maternal help and "the more closely adhere to the Mediator and Redeemer."

I recommend that you and your wife listen to the tape series, "The Biblical Understanding of Mary," by Scott Hahn, a Catholic with a Protestant background. He answers many of the common questions fundamentalists (and many Catholics) ask about Mary. The four-tape series may be ordered from St. Joseph Communications, 1-800-526-2151, outside California; and (818) 331-3549, in California.

Q Are angels real? No one seems to know much about them.

A Angels do exist. The Catholic Church teaches that God created invisible spirits called angels before the creation of the visible world. Angels are personal beings possessing understanding and free will. According to St. Gregory the Great, the word "angel" "denotes a function rather than a nature. Those holy spirits of heaven have always been spirits, but they can only be called angels when they deliver some message. Those who deliver messages of lesser importance are called angels, while those who proclaim messages of supreme importance are called archangels."

Angels play a big role in many familiar Bible stories. By one count, they appear explicitly 148 times in the Old Testament and 74 in the New Testament. Michael, Gabriel, and Raphael are the only three angels called by name in Scripture.

The doctrine that each person has an angel assigned to watch over and intercede for him or her, a "guardian" angel, is a long-standing tradition in the Church, but it has never been defined as an article of faith.

I strongly recommend that you read *O Angel of God, My Guardian Dear*, a collection of Pope John Paul II's talks on angels, which he gave in Rome in 1986. You can purchase the booklet from the National Center for Padre Pio, R.D. #1, Box 134, Old Route 100, Barto, Pennsylvania 19504; phone: (610) 845-3000.

Q At the last couple of funerals I've attended, the priests have preached about the deceased as if he or she were already in heaven. I don't mean to be disrespectful, but the deceased were not remarkably holy people. Do all Christians go to heaven when they die, or only the ones who are saints?

A We cannot say that all Christians immediately experience heaven after death. We cannot make a judgment reserved only to God. We must trust in his infinite mercy and remember the deceased at Mass and in our private prayers. It is possible that the soul of the deceased may be undergoing a final process of purification (purgatory), which will result in his eventual entry into the full glory of heaven. The Roman Catholic Church has a procedure called "canonization," for acknowledging and confirming the presence in heaven of men and women who have led lives of exemplary holiness. These are the people whom Catholics formally recognize as saints.

Barring canonization, we can't know the eternal destiny of the deceased. Remembering them at the Table of the Lord and in our private devotion is a time-honored and consoling tradition. Honoring a person at his funeral is perfectly acceptable as long as we do not "canonize" the person in our enthusiasm or eagerness to give comfort to the bereaved.

Q Protestant denominations seem to stress the need for conversion (that is, being "born again") at their weekly services. Why is it that many Catholics only hear about radical conversion on Cursillo weekends, Life in the Spirit Seminars, or through other renewal movements?

A It troubles me also that some of our priests don't even mention conversion unless we're in the season of Lent or participating in the groups you listed. They presuppose that everybody has a good relationship with the Lord. Though that is not the official posture of the Catholic Church, it's a prevalent viewpoint.

I agree with you that we should preach the need to turn to the Lord and be converted in mind and heart at every eucharistic gathering. We do that in the Penitential Rite of the Mass, but we need to emphasize it more in our preaching, giving people more opportunities to turn to the Lord.

While priests have a primary role in calling people to conversion, the laity also must share in the Church's mission of evangelization. "The very witness of a Christian life, and good works done in a supernatural spirit, are effective in drawing men to the faith and to God…. This witness of life, however, is not the sole element in the apostolate; the true apostle is on the lookout for occasions of announcing Christ by word, either to unbelievers to draw them toward the faith, or to the faithful to instruct them, strengthen them, incite them to a more fervent life" (*Apostolicam Actuositatem,* "Decree on the Apostolate of Lay People," No. 6).

Q I am a high school sophomore. I often feel cornered when my friends question me about my Catholic beliefs. What resources might help me talk to them about my faith?

A You could start with *Catholic and Christian,* and then move on to *Basics of the Faith: A Catholic Catechism.* Both of these books by Dr. Alan Schreck will give you a good foundation in the teachings of the Catholic Church. They can be ordered from Servant Publications, P.O. Box 8617, Ann Arbor, Michigan 48107; phone: (313) 761-8505.

I also recommend *You!* magazine, a publication for Catholic youth that is designed to help teens grow in knowledge and appreciation of their faith. You may order a free trial copy by writing to *You!,* 31194 La Baya Drive, Westlake Village, California 91362; phone: 1-800-359-0177.

Q What made it possible for St. Joachim and St. Anne not to pass on original sin to Mary?

A As is made clear in Pope Pius IX's official definition of the Immaculate Conception of Mary, only God's intervention made it possible for Mary to be conceived without original sin: "The most Blessed Virgin Mary, in the first instance of her conception, *by a singular grace and privilege granted by Almighty God,* in view of the merits of Jesus Christ, the Savior of the human race, was preserved free from all stain of original sin" [emphasis mine] (December 8, 1854).

"Although as a descendant of Adam in a sinful human race Mary would naturally have incurred the guilt of original sin, a special divine decree kept her free from it in light of the foreseen or anticipated merits of Jesus Christ" (*The Teaching of Christ*, Our Sunday Visitor). Dr. Alan Schreck explains it this way, "Mary actually was the first to be saved by the grace of her Son, Jesus. God first applied to Mary the grace that he knew and foresaw that Jesus would gain by his life and death on the cross" (*Basics of the Faith*, Servant).

Thus, the fact that Mary was conceived without original sin had nothing to do with the sanctity of her parents or her own holiness, but everything to do with God's plan for the salvation of the world.

Q Please explain the difference between the Catholic doctrine of transubstantiation and the Lutheran doctrine of consubstantiation.

A There is a real difference between the two doctrines. I'll try to explain them here simply, and then recommend some resources for further study.

Martin Luther, the sixteenth-century reformer, believed in consubstantiation, the theory that after the bread and wine are consecrated they coexist with the body and blood of Christ in the Eucharist.

The Catholic Church upholds the doctrine of transubstantiation, which states that the substance of the bread and wine are completely changed into the body and blood of Christ. Only the outward appearances of the bread and wine remain.

In the sixteenth century, the Council of Trent affirmed the doctrine of transubstantiation in these words: "Because Christ our Redeemer said that it was truly his body that he was offering under the species of bread (see Mt 26:26ff; Mk 14:22ff; Lk 22:19ff; 1 Cor 11:23ff), it has always been the conviction of the Church of God, and this holy Council now again declares that, by the consecration of the bread and wine there takes place a change of the whole substance of bread into the substance of the body of Christ our Lord and of the whole substance of wine into the substance of his blood. This change the holy Catholic Church has fittingly and properly named transubstantiation."

The Gospels of Matthew, Mark, and Luke all contain accounts of Jesus' giving himself under the species of bread and wine. The words of the consecration in the Mass come from 1 Corinthians 11, where Paul writes that the Lord "took bread, and after he had given thanks, broke it and said, 'This is my body, which is for you. Do this in remembrance of me.' In the same way, after the supper, he took the cup, saying, 'This cup is the new covenant in my blood. Do this, whenever you drink it, in remembrance of me.' "

The Teaching of Christ (Our Sunday Visitor) has a very good chapter on the Eucharist, and Dr. Alan Schreck's *Catholic and Christian* (Servant) gives a clear explanation of transubstantiation.

Q As a youngster in elementary school I was taught that Christ's vicar on earth, our Holy Father the Pope, and his teachings are infallible. Lately some of my Catholic friends have been challenging this point. What is the Church's teaching on papal infallibility?

A In Catholic teaching "infallibility" is understood as that gift of God that protects the Church of Jesus Christ from basically erring in matters of faith and morals. It is a guarantee resulting from the ongoing activity of the Holy Spirit within the Church community as promised by Jesus: "I have much more to tell you but you cannot bear it now. When he comes, however, being the Spirit of truth he will guide you to all truth" (Jn 16:12-13).

There are three aspects of infallibility that continue to be discussed by theologians: the infallibility of the Church; the infallibility of the college of bishops; and the infallibility of the pope. Here I shall focus on the infallibility of the pope, though in fact there is only one charism of infallibility in the Church.

The new *Code of Canon Law* expresses Catholic belief about the infallibility associated with the office and ministry of Peter in this way:

"The Supreme Pontiff, in virtue of his office, possesses infallible teaching authority when, as supreme pastor and teacher of all the faithful, whose task is to confirm his fellow believers in the faith, he proclaims with a definitive act that a doctrine of faith or morals is to be held as such" (Canon 749).

In his book *Catholic and Christian* (Servant), Dr. Alan Schreck thoroughly explains the history of the development of this doctrine. He states that for a papal teaching to be considered infallible it must meet these criteria: 1) The pope must be speaking *ex cathedra,* that is, "from the chair" of Peter, which means he must be speaking officially as the universal teacher and shepherd of all Catholic Christians as the successor of St. Peter; 2) The pope must clearly define the doctrine as being a truth of faith necessary for salvation; 3) It must be a definition concerning "faith or morals."

Two examples of infallible papal teachings are the 1854 doctrine of the Immaculate Conception of Mary and the 1950 doctrine of the Assumption of Mary into heaven.

The *New Catholic Encyclopedia* (McGraw-Hill) has a very informative article ("Infallibility," Vol. 7) on the contemporary view of papal infallibility. It points out that papal infallibility is neither absolute, personal, nor separate. Absolute infallibility belongs to God alone. Papal infallibility is limited to matters of faith and morals and extends only to the deposit of revelation. It is the Magisterium of the pope, that is, the teaching ministry of the bishop of Rome, the successor of St. Peter, that is infallible, not the private person of the man in office. Papal infallibility is grounded in the infallibility of the Church and is in relationship to the infallibility of the college of bishops.

The bishop of Rome, as universal pastor of all Catholic Christians, must use all the means available to search out the truth, not the least of which is consultation with other believers, especially bishops and theologians. The Second Vatican Council stated: "The holy people of God shares also in Christ's prophetic office.... The whole body of the faithful who have an anointing that comes from the Holy One cannot err in matters of belief" ("Dogmatic Constitution on the Church," No. 12).

Catholic Christians should have a graced attitude called *sentire cum ecclesia*. This means to desire that one's thinking, one's opinion, one's attitude, and therefore, even one's emotions be in line with the thinking of the Church as enunciated by the pope, the Second Vatican Council, and the Magisterium of our bishops.

The understanding of this safeguard of infallibility is still unfolding and developing as theologians reflect upon the Tradition. While the exercise of this charism is rare, it is part of Catholic doctrine. Of more importance is the acceptance and life application of the ordinary, everyday teachings of our pope and national conferences of bishops, which are designed to disciple us and form us as modern-day followers of Jesus Christ. I believe there should be more assent to these teachings than the so-often publicized dissent in the Church.

As Catholics we can enjoy the security and sense of well-being that comes from knowing that the Holy Spirit is guiding the Magisterium of our Church, and that we can trust in the reliability of those instructions and teachings on faith and morals that come from our pope and our national conferences of bishops, especially when they agree in council.

Q Has there been a change in the Church's teaching about life immediately after death and before the final resurrection? Some of the prayers in the new Rite of Funerals seem to give the image of the deceased sleeping in the grave until awakened to glory.

A I share a similar concern about some of the prayers in our new ritual book. We must understand the biblical imagery on which those prayers are based in light of the Tradition clarified in the 1979 instruction, "The Reality of Life After Death," issued by the Sacred Congregation for the Doctrine of the Faith with the approval of Pope John Paul II:

"The Church affirms that a spiritual element survives and subsists after death, an element endowed with consciousness and will, so that the 'human self' subsists. To designate this element, the Church uses the word 'soul,' the accepted term in the usage of Scripture and Tradition."

The instruction goes on to affirm the Catholic Church's belief in a future resurrection that is "distinct and deferred with respect to the situation of people immediately after death."

Thus, there will be a marvelous moment in the unfolding of history when "the whole person" will share in the Resurrection of Jesus Christ. Until then, the soul lives on, awaiting the time of fulfillment.

Despite a modern liberal tendency to the contrary, there is no change in the traditional teaching about heaven, hell, and purgatory.

The instruction states: "The Church believes in the happiness of the just who will one day be with Christ. She believes that there will be eternal punishment for the sinner, who will be deprived of the sight of God, and that this punishment will have a repercussion on the whole being of the sinner. She believes in the possibility of a purification for the elect before they see God, a purification altogether different from the punishment of the damned."

The Church admits, "Neither Scripture nor theology provides sufficient light for a proper picture of life after death." On the other hand, the document says, "Respect must, however, be given to the images employed in the Scriptures." I believe anyone who is walking with Christ and anointed with the Holy Spirit will draw great consolation and inspiration from the "images employed in the Scriptures."

The instruction states that Christians must firmly hold these essential points: "They must believe in the fundamental continuity, thanks to the power of the Holy Spirit, between our present life in Christ and the future life," and yet, "they must be clearly aware of the radical break between the present life and the future one, due to the fact that the economy of faith will be replaced by the economy of fullness of life."

I myself, in pondering the awesomeness of dying and the challenge of daily living, draw great encouragement from the wisdom of the word of God: "Eye has not seen, ear has not heard, nor has it so much as dawned on man what God has prepared for those who love him" (1 Cor 2:9).

There is also great consolation in our Catholic practice of remembering the deceased at the Table of the Lord, that is, at holy Mass. Our prayers can assist those who may be undergoing purgation. The Eucharist unites us more profoundly to the risen Lord, through whom we still have a relationship with those "who have gone before us" (Eucharistic Prayer, No. 1). With them, we too await the glorious manifestation of our Lord Jesus Christ" when there will be established "new heavens and a new earth" (Rev 21:1).

Then, as we now so long, "There shall be no more death or mourning, crying out or pain" (Rev 21:4).

You may find the research done by Raymond A. Moody in his volumes titled *Life After Life* (Bantam Books) very interesting. Such clinical death experiences somewhat verify what our faith teaches, namely, we do meet the Lord in the human death process. Then comes a particular or individual judgment even as we await the general and final judgment. May we all be prepared for that day by living a good and holy life in Christ Jesus.

Chapter VI: Sexuality

Q Is masturbation ever an acceptable practice to relieve sexual tension? Different priests have given me conflicting answers on this.

A Many Catholics today, including some priests, doubt or deny the traditional teaching of the Church that masturbation is objectively a grave sin. To reaffirm this and other traditional teachings, the Sacred Congregation for the Doctrine of the Faith issued the "Declaration on Certain Problems of Sexual Ethics" in 1975.

It states, "Whatever force there may be in certain biological and philosophical arguments put forward from time to time by theologians, the fact remains that both the Magisterium of the Church, in the course of a constant Tradition, and the moral sense of the faithful have been in no doubt and have firmly maintained that masturbation is an intrinsically and gravely disordered action. The principal argument in support of this truth is that the deliberate use of the sexual faculty, for whatever reason, outside of marriage is essentially contrary to its purpose. For it lacks that sexual relationship demanded by the moral order and in which 'the total meaning of mutual self-giving and human procreation in the context of true love' is achieved. All deliberate sexual activity must therefore be referred to the married state" (No. 9).

The Declaration further states, "Although it cannot be established that Sacred Scripture condemned masturbation by name, the tradition of the Church has rightly taken it to have been condemned by the New Testament when it speaks of 'uncleanness' and 'unchastity' and other vices contrary to chastity and continence" (No. 9).

The Church admits that "modern psychology has much that is valid and useful to offer on the subject of masturbation. It is helpful for gauging moral responsibility more accurately and for directing pastoral activity along the right lines. It can enable one to understand how adolescent immaturity, which sometimes lasts beyond adolescence, the lack of psychological balance, and ingrained habit can influence a person's behavior, diminishing his responsibility for his actions, with the result that he is not always guilty of subjectively grave fault" (No. 9).

To have pastoral compassion toward one struggling with the habit of masturbation is one thing. To condone, approve, and even suggest such a practice is normal is another. Such a stance is contrary to the truth and scandalous, misleading many who should rather be led "by means of a complete education, to proper mental, affective, and moral maturity" (No. 13).

In Catholic Sexual Ethics: A Summary, Explanation, & Defense (Our Sunday Visitor), the authors explain the heart of the Church's teaching on the immorality of masturbation: "From St. Paul (1 Thes 4:1-5, 1 Cor 6:15-20) Christians have learned that their bodies are the temples of the Holy Spirit, that their flesh has become one with the flesh of Christ. Our genital organs, Christians have thus rightly concluded, are not playthings or tools that we are to employ simply for pleasure. Rather, they are integral to our persons, and our free choice to exercise our genital powers is thus to be in service of human persons. The goods to which sexual activity is ordered … include procreation, marital friendship, and chaste self-possession. By respecting these goods when we use our genital powers, we honor the body that has, through baptism, become one body with Christ and a temple of his Spirit. When we do not respect these goods in our genital activity we act immorally, and we desecrate the temple of the Holy Spirit and abuse the bodyperson who has been purchased at such great price" (Chapter 8).

I recommend the "Declaration on Certain Problems of Sexual Ethics" for your further study. This profound document may be found in Eerdmans' *Vatican Council II: The Conciliar and Post Conciliar Documents* (Volume II), edited by Austin Flannery, O.P.

Q When is the Catholic Church going to shed its antiquated laws about sexuality? Those rules serve no purpose but to make people feel guilty and inhibited about a God-given gift.

A People who can easily see the need for gun control laws and highway safety laws to protect human life often can't see the need for moral laws protecting the dignity of persons and safeguarding the sanctity of marriage and family life.

The so-called sexual revolution, which threw off traditional sexual morality in its bid for freedom, has only proved the need for the Church's "antiquated laws." The rampant hedonism that resulted reduced human beings to the status of objects and ushered in an unmatched time of misery and sexual confusion. The statistics on the increase in adultery, premarital sex, divorce, rape, incest, sexual abuse, pornography, homosexuality, contraception, and other ills are simply staggering.

I believe now is the time to proclaim even more energetically the truth of the Catholic Church's teaching on human sexuality. This teaching, based as it is on divine and natural law, is indeed ancient, but the truth never goes out of style.

Contrary to the belief that the Catholic Church views sexuality as something dirty and shameful, the Church teaches that physical intimacy between spouses is indeed a beautiful, pleasurable, sacred gift from God. Since the positive aspect of Church teaching on sexuality gets so little press, I include here quotes from several Church documents:

"Sexuality, by means of which man and woman give

themselves to one another through the acts which are proper and exclusive to spouses, is by no means something purely biological, but concerns the innermost being of the human person as such. It is realized in a truly human way only if it is an integral part of the love by which a man and a woman commit themselves totally to one another until death. The total physical self-giving would be a lie if it were not the sign and fruit of a total personal self-giving" (*Familiaris Consortio*, "The Christian Family in the Modern World," No. 11).

" 'The acts in marriage by which the intimate and chaste union of the spouses takes place are noble and honorable; the truly human performance of these acts fosters the self-giving they signify and enriches the spouses in joy and gratitude.' Sexuality is a source of joy and pleasure: 'The Creator himself … established that in the [generative] function, spouses should experience pleasure and enjoyment of body and spirit. Therefore, the spouses do nothing evil in seeking this pleasure and enjoyment. They accept what the Creator has intended for them. At the same time, spouses should know how to keep themselves within the limits of just moderation' " (*Catechism of the Catholic Church*, No. 2362).

"There are some who would allege that happiness in marriage is in direct proportion to the reciprocal enjoyment in conjugal relations. It is not so: indeed, happiness in marriage is in direct proportion to the mutual respect of the partners, even in their intimate relations; not that they regard as immoral and refuse what nature offers and what the Creator has given, but because this respect, and the mutual esteem which it produces, is one of the strongest elements of a pure love, and for this reason all the more tender" (Pope Pius XII, "Allocution to Midwives," 1951).

"Love must be protected by the stability of marriage if sexual intercourse is really to meet the demands of its own finality and of human dignity. For this to be achieved there is need of a contract sanctioned and protected by society. The marriage contract inaugurates a state of life which is of the greatest importance. It makes possible a union between husband and wife that is exclusive and promotes the good of their family and of the whole of human society" ("Declaration on Certain Problems of Sexual Ethics," No. 7).

Chastity, modesty, and purity are essential components for understanding the awesome reality of human sexuality. In fact, the most healthy, wholesome, and profound wisdom about human sexuality is found within the authentic teachings of the Catholic Church. Mere information and biological data without moral principles and God's view of humanity leave people without the whole truth, which alone liberates and frees.

Q Is it true that the Catholic Church teaches homosexuality is a disorder? Hasn't modern psychology come to accept such behavior?

A The official teaching of the Catholic Church on homosexuality may be found in the Sacred Congregation for the Doctrine of the Faith's "Letter to the Bishops on the Pastoral Care of Homosexual Persons" (1985). The letter points out that some Catholics mistakenly give an overly benign interpretation to homosexual orientation, going so far as to consider such orientation neutral or even good. It has always been taught that homosexual genital activity is intrinsically disordered and therefore objectively gravely sinful.

The correct and clear teaching about such orientation is: "Although the particular inclination of the homosexual person is not a sin, it is a more or less strong tendency ordered toward an intrinsic moral evil; and thus the inclination itself must be seen as an objective disorder. Therefore special concern and pastoral attention should be directed toward those who have this condition, lest they be led to believe that the living out of this orientation in homosexual activity is a morally acceptable option. It is not."

Most recently the same Congregation issued a letter entitled "Some Considerations Concerning the Catholic Response to Legislative Proposals on the Non-Discrimination of Homosexual Persons." Both documents are available in any good library or from publications like *Origins* or *Crux*.

The official position of the Church, which is filled with truth and compassion, should be studied and understood by those sensitive to this issue. In 1986 the letter from the Congregation was followed up in *L'Osservatore Romano* with some very profound psychological analysis supporting the Church's position.

We must try to take on the mind and attitude of Jesus toward any person struggling with psychosexual disorders, be they heterosexual or homosexual, as we seek to help others live lives of wholesome chastity and self-control. The activity of the Holy Spirit is absolutely essential in the maturation process toward wholesome and integrated sexuality.

Finally we must note that "it is deplorable that homosexual persons have been and are the object of violent malice in speech or in action. Such treatment deserves condemnation from the Church's pastors wherever it occurs. It reveals a kind of disregard for others that endangers the most fundamental principles of a healthy society. The intrinsic dignity of each person must always be respected in word, in action, and in law" ("Pastoral Care of Homosexual Persons").

Q While taking a premarriage course, my daughter was told that oral sex can be a part of the sexual act after marriage. Is that true?

A When oral stimulation of the husband's genitals by the wife causes his ejaculation (orgasm) to happen outside of her vagina, it is gravely wrong and is *not* permitted morally. Such stimulation by his wife, which does not lead to his climax outside of her vagina, and which is part of a completed act of normal genital intercourse, is permitted. Therefore, as a method of foreplay and lovemaking, and as part of normal and natural genital-genital intercourse, such stimulation is morally acceptable.

Oral stimulation of the wife's genitalia by her husband is permitted during sexual lovemaking, even to the point of feminine orgasm if at some time during the expression of love there is normal and natural vaginal intercourse as nature and God intend.

Partners should not engage in oral stimulation if such activity is repugnant to either one.

The Catholic Church's concern with this form of sexual expression is rooted in the nature of the conjugal act of love, which must always allow for the transmission of life as taught by the Church. When oral sex is not part of a completed act of genital-genital intercourse, it becomes a means of contraception. You will notice I make a clear distinction between oral stimulation in association with natural intercourse and just plain oral intercourse. Oral intercourse involving a husband's ejaculation outside of his wife's vagina is objectively a grave disorder, seriously sinful and unnatural.

Q Can you recommend any good Christian books for those struggling with homosexuality?

A Father John Harvey, O.S.F.S., is the founder of Courage, an organization that provides personal and spiritual support to Catholic homosexual men and women who are trying to live chaste lives. He also founded a support group for relatives of homosexuals. Father Harvey's excellent book entitled *The Homosexual Person: New Thinking in Pastoral Care* (Ignatius Press) provides good solid information rooted in the Church's teaching on homosexuality.

Father Harvey, who has some forty years experience in the pastoral care of homosexual persons, also recommends the following: *The Courage to Be Chaste* (Paulist) by Father Benedict Groeschel, C.F.R., which is an excellent treatment of the homosexual person's struggle for chastity; *Psychogenesis* (Routledge and Kegan Paul, Ltd.) and *Homosexuality* (Attic Press) by Dr. Elizabeth Moberly; *The Broken Image* (Crossway Books) by Leanne Payne; *Homosexuality and Hope* (Servant) by Gerard van den Aardweg; and *Homosexuality: The Questions* (St. Paul Books and Media) by Joseph A. DiIenno, M.D. and Father Herbert F. Smith, S.J., which has an excellent annotated bibliography that would be helpful to anyone interested in the subject.

In case you're interested, the address for Courage is St. Michael's Rectory, 424 W. 34th Street, New York, New York 10001.

Q There seems to be a lot of confusion about Catholic Church teaching on birth control. What is the Church's position on this issue?

A In 1981, Pope John Paul II clearly reaffirmed the Church's teaching: that "love between husband and wife must be fully human, exclusive, and open to new life" (*Familiaris Consortio*, "The Christian Family in the Modern World," No. 29).

This clear moral teaching has also been set forth in Vatican II's *Gaudium et Spes* ("Pastoral Constitution on the Church in the Modern World," No. 50), and in Pope Paul VI's encyclical *Humanae Vitae* ("On the Regulation of Birth"). To summarize: "The Church, calling men back to the observance of the norms of the natural law, as interpreted by its constant doctrine, teaches that each and every marriage act must remain open to the transmission of life" (*Humanae Vitae*, No. 11). Thus, all forms of artificial contraception, directly willed and procured abortion, and direct sterilization of either man or woman are forbidden.

Confusion results from the social and cultural conditions of our age that do not support such a teaching. A very strong anti-life mentality exists in our world

Confusion also results because most other Christian churches do not agree with the consistent, unchanging moral doctrine of the Catholic Church on this issue. Until about the middle of this century, there was unanimity of thought among all Christian groups on life issues, but since then, most mainline Protestant churches have opted for a more liberal stance.

Further confusion has been caused by vocal dissent by a significant number of Catholic clergy, religious, and laity against the Magisterium's teachings that forbid interfering with the generative process of conjugal sexual intercourse. To counteract this confusion, Pope John Paul II has urgently and pressingly asked theologians "to unite their efforts in order to collaborate with the hierarchical Magisterium and to commit themselves to the task of illustrating ever more clearly the biblical foundations, the ethical grounds, and the personalistic reasons behind this doctrine" (*Familiaris Consortio*, No. 31).

Pope Paul VI predicted grave consequences to our world if a contraceptive mentality prevailed over and against the Church's teachings. He warned of an increase in conjugal infidelity and a general lowering of morality. I believe his encyclical was prophetic. I would advise all who care for the Church and the world we live in to read *Humanae Vitae* again, and to assent wholeheartedly to the wisdom it contains.

The Catholic Church advocates responsible natural family planning as distinguished from artificial birth control. For information on morally acceptable birth regulation, I refer our readers to the Couple-to-Couple League, P.O. Box 111184, Cincinnati, Ohio 45211, (513) 661-7612.

The Church also recognizes the difficulty some married couples may have in living out these teachings. In the words of Pope Paul VI: "Let them implore divine assistance by persevering prayer; above all, let them draw from the source of grace and charity in the Eucharist. And if sin should still keep its hold over them, let them not be discouraged, but rather have recourse with humble perseverance to the mercy of God, which is poured forth in the sacrament of penance" (*Humanae Vitae*, No. 25).

Q Is genital foreplay ever acceptable for those who are not married? I get very different answers from priests in my area.

A Common sense and the Church's teaching on self-control of our sexual drives (chastity) seem to provide compelling reasons to avoid genital foreplay. Foreplay by definition is "erotic stimulation preceding sexual intercourse." The Catholic Church teaches that sexual intercourse may take place only within the covenant of marriage. Expressions of love and affection before marriage should avoid activity that naturally and biologically impels toward full sexual intercourse.

Chastity educator Molly Kelly explains it this way to her teen audiences: "You never go out to the driveway, get in the car, turn on the motor, rev it up, turn it off, and go back in the house. If you rev the motor up, you usually intend to go someplace. If you rev one another up, it's difficult to stop."

Modesty and healthy reserve, while not encouraged by the world, are in the best of the Christian tradition. Certain touches and expressions of affection, especially involving the genital areas, are to be reserved for the season of love that will be yours when you are married.

I strongly recommend that you and your boyfriend help one another protect the precious gift of human sexuality by growing in the virtue of chastity. Living a chaste life may seem impossible in a society obsessed with sex, but by God's grace it can be done. Remember, "God keeps his promise. He will not let you be tested beyond your strength. Along with the test he will give you a way out of it so that you may be able to endure it" (1 Cor 10:13).

In its "Declaration on Certain Problems of Sexual Ethics" (1975), the Sacred Congregation for the Doctrine of the Faith urged Christians to use the means recommended by the Church for living chastely: "They are: discipline of the senses and of the mind, vigilance and prudence in avoiding occasions of sin, modesty, moderation in amusements, wholesome pursuits, constant prayer, and frequent recourse to the sacraments of penance and the Eucharist. Young people especially should diligently develop devotion to the Immaculate Mother of God and should take as models the lives of the saints and of other Christians, especially young Christians who excelled in the practice of chastity.

"It is particularly important that everyone should hold the virtue of chastity in high esteem, its beauty and its radiant splendor. This virtue emphasizes man's dignity and opens man to a love that is true, magnanimous, unselfish, and respectful of others" (No. 12).

This is what Scripture teaches: "As for lewd conduct or promiscuousness or lust of any sort, let them not even be mentioned among you; your holiness forbids this" (Eph 5:3).

Q My fiancé and I are preparing to get married, and we were wondering if you could recommend any reading materials explaining the Catholic Church's teaching on sexuality.

A I would first advise you to read the "Declaration on Certain Problems of Sexual Ethics" (1975). Ralph Martin's book, *Husbands, Wives, Parents, Children* (Servant), has outstanding chapters on sexuality and gives a good overall understanding of the foundations of a Catholic Christian marriage relationship. The Couple-to-Couple League, P.O. Box 111184, Cincinnati, Ohio 45211 offers literature on natural family planning and its application.

Chapter VII: Piety

Q Is it valid to use blessed salt for prayer against evil spirits? Is this a sacramental like many others? Can anyone use it?

A Until the revision of the ceremonies for baptism in 1969, a small quantity of salt was placed in the mouth of the one being baptized. This rite was most likely a transformation of an ancient Roman custom of sprinkling salt on the lips of children on the eighth day after their birth. The Romans believed salt had an exorcising and cleansing effect.

Christians adopted salt for liturgical use because of its preservative qualities and as a sign of purity, permanence, and wisdom. Both Christ's words, "You are the salt of the earth" (Mt 5:13), and St. Paul's urging, "Let your speech always be gracious, seasoned with salt, so that you may know how you ought to answer everyone" (Col 4:6 RSV) are also believed to have influenced the introduction of salt into liturgy.

Today, when the Rite of Blessing and Sprinkling with Holy Water is used at Mass in place of the Penitential Rite, salt may be blessed and then mixed with holy water. As the priest blesses the salt he prays, "Wherever this salt and water are sprinkled, drive away the power of evil, and protect us always by the presence of your Holy Spirit."

As this brief history indicates, salt has long been associated with prayer against evil spirits. It may, like blessed oil or holy water, be used by lay people as a sacramental, provided it is "treated with reverence" and is not "employed for improper or profane use" (*Code of Canon Law*, Canon 1171).

Sacramentals, which are not to be confused with sacraments, are defined in Canon 1166 as "sacred signs by which spiritual effects especially are signified and are obtained by the intercession of the Church."

I personally make use of holy water and blessed salt as a protection against evil. I believe this is in keeping with the best of Catholic Christian tradition. The official prayers of the Roman Rite as indicated above testify to the spiritual power of such a practice.

Q I know that as a Catholic, I should respect Mary as the Mother of God. However, I have a problem with many excesses I've seen in Marian devotion. Is there a balanced approach to honoring Mary?

A The official teaching of the Catholic Church on Marian devotion is balanced, but because of ignorance of that teaching or excessive zeal, some forms of Marian devotion can displace the honor due to God alone.

The Church teaches that only God — the Father, Son, and Holy Spirit — is to be worshiped and adored. Other human beings can be admired, appreciated, loved, and honored for the holiness of their Christian lives and asked to intercede for us, but only God is to receive our absolute worship and adoration.

Catholics have always had a very strong appreciation of the role of Mary. She is honored for her special place in Scripture and her unique role in salvation history as the Mother of our Lord Jesus Christ. Out of love for Jesus, Catholics attempt to confer on her the same love and honor that God himself conferred on her in choosing her as the Mother of his only Son, the Savior of the human race. When we invoke the intercession of Mary, we are actually asking her to join us in praying to God who alone can answer our prayers. All of our prayers are answered only through Jesus our Lord, our one mediator (see 1 Tim 2:5). Thus, invoking Mary's prayers for us now and at the hour of our death does not contain any aspect of worship or adoration.

As with all customs, even those strongly rooted in Scripture, abuses have arisen at certain times in the history of the Church. The Vatican II Fathers strongly urged "theologians and preachers of the word of God to be careful to refrain as much from all false exaggeration as from too summary an attitude in considering the special dignity of the Mother of God" ("Dogmatic Constitution on the Church," No. 67).

Whenever abuses or incorrect understandings do occur, theologians and preachers are called to explain them and to lead us to a healthy, joyful appreciation of our rich heritage in the Roman Catholic Church.

Q I'd like to do more to evangelize others, but I worry that they'll think I'm putting them down for not knowing Christ. How can I share the gospel without sounding like I have a "holier-than-thou" attitude?

A Your aim as an evangelist is to serve the other person by sharing the good news of Jesus Christ. When you know that you are to be servant — not judge, not savior, not counselor — it's easier to avoid sounding superior.

Keep your witness simple, and focus on Jesus Christ. Talk about your experience of him and how you look to him as *your* Savior in the midst of your weaknesses.

Remember that the way you say things can be just as important as what you say. Approach the person with awe, knowing that even before he comes to Christ, by the very fact of his humanity, he is entitled to unconditional love and absolute respect. You'll find that idea in Scripture and see it repeated many times in the teachings of Pope John Paul II, who strongly emphasizes the dignity of the individual person.

Listening is one way to show that profound respect; your tone of voice and bodily posture can also communicate it.

Sometimes, despite your best intentions, you will be misunderstood. If you're accused of having a "holier-than-thou" attitude, you should simply reflect the accusation and say, "I'm sorry if that's your perception. I don't mean to come across that way. But I do know One who is holier than both of us, and his name is Jesus Christ."

Never let anyone deter you — even with accusation or judgment — from proclaiming Jesus Christ.

Q I sometimes wonder about the proliferation of relics. It seems impossible that there can be so many thousands of relics from one saint. Please comment.

A Relics are divided into three categories: First-class relics are part of the saint's body, second-class relics are clothing or other articles used by the saint during his life, and third-class relics are any other object that has been touched to a first-class relic.

Obviously, first- and second-class relics are rare, but there can indeed be an unlimited number of third-class relics.

Relics — from the Latin *"reliquiae,"* meaning remains — have been venerated since the early days of the Church. Just as we often keep a special possession belonging to a deceased loved one to remind us of that person, so the early Christians preserved the bodies and possessions of the saints and martyrs. The first non-scriptural reference to relics is found in a 156 A.D. account of the martyrdom of St. Polycarp. By the tenth century it had become common to house relics in churches or shrines, a practice that continues today.

Joan Carroll Cruz's book, *Relics* (Our Sunday Visitor), provides photos and some very interesting historical and theological details about many relics venerated by Catholics today. To order a copy, call 1-800-348-2440.

Q I really dislike fasting, yet I know many people who fast every week, whether it's Lent or not. Can you help me understand the importance of this practice in the spiritual life?

A The Catholic Church has always taught that self-denial is an important means to union with God. Fasting helps us to reorder our priorities, to remember that God, not food, is first in our lives. Fasting intensifies our efforts as intercessors by allowing us more time and attention for prayer. Fasting can also enable us to hear the word of God better when we are looking for guidance.

Scripture is full of references to fasting, which describe various ways and means and times for fasting. For starters, you could read Isaiah 58:1-14; Joel 1:14; 2:12; Luke 4:2; Acts 13:2-3; 14:23; and Matthew 6:16-18; 17:21.

Some people dislike fasting because it can cause headaches or other health problems. Fasting doesn't have to mean consuming absolutely no food or water; adjustments can be made. For example, a bread and water fast can be done instead of a complete fast. Fruit juice or milk can be substituted for water. And if you are unable to fast from food, other acts of self-discipline or charity can be joined to your prayers. In any case, it is the spirit in which the fast is undertaken that is most important. A humbled, contrite heart will do much to advance God's cause in our day.

Q What is the present discipline of the Catholic Church regarding fasting and abstaining from meat, especially during Lent?

A Fasting and abstinence are part of a long Christian tradition that began with Jesus Christ himself.

Fasting is a "form of penance that imposes limits on the kind or quantity of food or drink" (*Modern Catholic Dictionary*, Doubleday). Though he had no need of personal repentance,

Jesus "fasted for forty days and forty nights" (Mt 4:2). He also taught his disciples how to fast (see Mt 6:16-18) and told detractors his disciples would fast "when the Bridegroom is taken away" (Mk 2:18-20). We also find many occasions when the apostles fasted in the New Testament (see Acts 13:2; 14:23). Following this example, the earliest Christians observed weekly fast days (usually Wednesdays and Fridays).

According to the *New Catholic Encyclopedia*, abstinence — refraining from certain kinds of food or drink, especially flesh meats — was early established, and "the observance of the Friday abstinence in commemoration of the Passion and Death of Our Lord was common in both the Eastern and Western Church."

Though Catholics may, of course, fast and abstain from meat or other foods at other times, the Church has marked Ash Wednesday, Fridays in Lent, and the Friday of the Passion and Death of our Lord Jesus Christ as special days of penance.

In their pastoral statement of November 18, 1966, the National Conference of Catholic Bishops determined the following:

"Catholics in the United States are obliged to abstain from the eating of meat on Ash Wednesday and on all Fridays during the season of Lent. They are obliged to fast on Ash Wednesday and on Good Friday. Self-imposed observance of fasting on all weekdays of Lent is strongly recommended. Abstinence from flesh meat on all Fridays of the year is especially recommended to individuals and to the Catholic community as a whole."

The current discipline defines fasting as one full meal and two lighter meals in the course of a day.

Canon 1252 of the *Code of Canon Law* states, "All persons who have completed their fourteenth year are bound by the law of abstinence; all adults are bound by the law of fast up to the beginning of their sixtieth year. Nevertheless, pastors and parents are to see to it that minors who are not bound by the law of fast and abstinence are educated in an authentic sense of penance."

Canon 1249 says, "In order that all may be joined in a common observance of penance, penitential days are prescribed in which the Christian faithful in a special way pray, exercise works of piety and charity, and deny themselves by fulfilling their responsibilities more faithfully and especially by observing fast and abstinence."

Those who are too young, too old, or too ill to observe these days of fast and abstinence are expected to substitute other works of penance, especially works of charity and exercises of piety, as they are able.

Q Why do we make the sign of the cross?

A The sign of the cross is an action by which Christians profess their belief in Jesus Christ's redemption of mankind by his Death on the cross and their belief in the Holy Trinity, God the Father, the Son, and the Holy Spirit.

According to Our Sunday Visitor's *Catholic Encyclopedia*, the early Church Father Tertullian (230 A.D.) attested to "the tracing of the sign of the cross on the forehead as a personal gesture of piety to sanctify the actions of daily life." It was also used early on in the rites of baptism and confirmation and later developed as a Mass gesture at the beginning and end of each liturgy.

The sign of the cross is regularly used as one begins and ends personal prayers and with holy water as one enters a church or chapel. It is a powerful religious gesture and should be used devoutly and reverently, both publicly and privately, by us who have been "marked with the sign of faith" (Roman Canon, No. 1).

As Blessed John Henry Newman says so beautifully in his poem, "The Sign of the Cross":
Whene'er across this sinful flesh of mine
I draw the Holy Sign,

All good thoughts stir within me, and renew
Their slumbering strength divine;
Till there springs up a courage high and true
To suffer and to do.

Q I've often wondered why my Catholic friends wear crucifixes as jewelry and why Catholic churches always seem to have crucifixes in them. Would you please explain this?

A Throughout the history of Christianity, crucifixes have served to inspire men and women of God to holiness, and for that reason the crucifix holds a central place in most Catholic churches. The crucifix, as a sign and symbol of Jesus' act of love and sacrifice that atoned for our sins, stirs our hearts to love our Savior all the more ardently and constantly calls our attention to him who alone saved us by his very own blood. Also a blessed cross serves as a sacramental that repels demonic spirits.

Catholics who wear a crucifix do not consider it a spiritual good luck charm. We don't believe there is any inherent power in the material out of which the crucifix was made. When we wear or look upon the crucifix, we are not worshiping the artist's representation of our crucified Savior, but the real Person of Jesus the figure reminds us of.

Looking upon a crucifix calls me to contemplate what our Savior accomplished for us upon the cross and what he suffered for our salvation.

Chapter VIII: Charismatic Renewal

Q At our prayer meeting, newcomers and people who prophesy infrequently must submit their prophesy in writing to a member of the word gift ministry. This rule has inhibited many people from giving prophecies. I'd appreciate your comments.

A I encourage you, if you haven't already, to speak to the prayer meeting leaders about your pastoral concerns. The rule does sound too restrictive to me, but the leaders may have reasons for it that you do not know about. Even St. Paul had rules of order governing prophesy (see 1 Cor 14).

Sometimes in the interest of safeguarding the integrity of the group, leadership can inadvertently legislate spiritual gifts too much. I would be inclined to let the whole body hear the prophecies and allow the testing to occur within the body. The more inspirational a prophesy, the less we have to be concerned about. The more directional a prophetic utterance, the more it needs to be tested.

If people feel uncomfortable with any prophecies that are given, they can bring their concerns to the attention of the leaders. If necessary, the leaders could address the problem at the next meeting.

I believe it's possible for newcomers to a group to have valid prophecies. We encourage those we are praying over to be baptized in the Spirit to yield to that gift if they are experiencing it. In general, I believe easing up on the restrictions allows people the freedom to develop the gift of prophesy.

Q I have been to several charismatic prayer meetings, but have yet to hear a good explanation of the gift of tongues. Can you help me understand this gift?

A Confusion often abounds over this "least of the gifts" of the Holy Spirit, which was written about in the New Testament and is now being experienced in the Church in this time of renewal.

Tongues is a prayer gift that can be public or private. In public prayer gatherings it is used for praise and sometimes in a prophetic word (which must be followed by an interpretation) to upbuild those assembled. In private prayer, tongues is used for praise and intercession. It is a valid spiritual gift that is usually experienced by those who have yielded to the action of the Holy Spirit in their lives.

A few Christian traditions hold that the gift of tongues is the actual sign of the Holy Spirit in a person's life and that you have not received the Holy Spirit until you pray in tongues. On the contrary, I believe that you can receive the Holy Spirit and not yield to or receive the gift of tongues. I personally pray in tongues and would love for all Christians to receive this special language of the heart to worship and honor God. But I do not feel that the gift of tongues is necessary for salvation, or that all Christians must pray in tongues. As with all the spiritual gifts or charisms, tongues should lead us to center not on ourselves or even on the gift itself, but to center upon loving and adoring the giver of all gifts, our Lord and Savior, Jesus Christ.

I would advise you to read *The Holy Spirit and You* (Bridge Publishing) by Dennis and Rita Bennett. It explains such matters as being baptized in the Holy Spirit, speaking in tongues, prophesy, healing, and so on. It is available through Charismatic Renewal Services: 1-800-348-2227.

Q You used the word "yield" in your answer to a question about the gift of tongues. It has been my experience that those who have not received the gift of tongues are looked down upon as somehow not yielding to the Holy Spirit. I resent the implication that I or others might not be yielding to the gift.

A It was not my intention to pass judgment on anyone who has not received the gift of tongues, and I regret that anyone would look down upon you because you do not pray in tongues.

The word "yield" is often used in explanations about the gift of tongues, because it accurately describes what many of us had to do in order to accept the gift. Either from a fear of experiencing this unusual manifestation of the Holy Spirit or a desire to control the kind of gifts we wanted from the Lord, we refused to yield our heart, mind, and tongue to the activity of the Holy Spirit. Once we surrendered freely to the Holy Spirit, we did receive the gift of tongues.

Because this is a common experience, I can understand why some people have come to believe that anyone who does not receive the gift of tongues is not yielding to the Lord. Many Catholics also subscribe to the belief held by some other Christians that tongues is the proof that one is baptized in the Holy Spirit. It is the Catholic Church's position, however, that praying in tongues is not the only manifestation of being baptized in the Holy Spirit.

It is the Holy Spirit's work and timing as to when or if we will receive that particular gift. St. Paul makes it clear that we all have different gifts: "To one the Spirit gives wisdom in discourse, to another the power to express knowledge. Through the Spirit one receives faith; by the same Spirit another is given the gift of healing, and still another miraculous powers. Prophesy is given to one; to another power to distinguish one spirit from another. One receives the gift of tongues, another that of interpreting the tongues. But it is one and the same Spirit who produces all these gifts, distributing them to each as he wills" (1 Cor 12:8-11).

I pray in tongues, and I delight in the gift. I would hope that all Christians would be open to such a prayer gift, but we ought not to make more out of it than the Scriptures do. I do not believe in inducing people to pray in tongues.

It is more important that you constantly and peacefully yield or surrender your life to the saving activity of the Holy Spirit.

Q Last week during our prayer meeting, I spontaneously led a Hail Mary after the Our Father we usually pray to conclude our time for worship. Several people later told me that they thought praying a Hail Mary was out of place in a prayer meeting. I think that Mary, as Mother of God, deserves to be honored any time Catholics meet for prayer. What do you think?

A I understand your love for Mary. I, too, have a loving appreciation of her unique role in our salvation, and I frequently pray the Rosary.

It is in the richest traditions of the Catholic Church's night prayer to acknowledge and honor Mary by saying the Hail Mary. In your situation, however, you need to handle the issue carefully so as not to be a source of conflict or alienation. Since not everyone in your group is in agreement about the appropriateness of honoring Mary, I think it would be wise to receive the approval of the prayer meeting leaders before introducing any changes in format.

If they decide to include a Hail Mary, they might introduce the change by offering a series of talks on the Church's authentic teaching on the role of Mary and how Christians should honor her. Such a series could lay to rest the concerns of the dissenting members and open the whole group to the graces obtained through Mary's intercession.

Q I've recently started a new job as a youth minister at our parish. Some of the kids have spoken to me about their involvement in the occult and Satanism. I feel the need to learn more about deliverance from evil spirits if I am going to help these teens. Do you know of any books on deliverance that might be useful in pastoral ministry?

A Three very good books are: *Deliverance from Evil Spirits* (Servant) by Father Michael Scanlan, T.O.R., and Randall J. Cirner; *Deliverance Prayer: Experiential, Psychological, and Theological Approaches* (Paulist Press) edited by Matthew and Dennis Linn, S.J.; and *Deliver Us from Evil* (Revell) by Don Basham.

You may order all three of these books and an updated catalog of other good literature from Charismatic Renewal Services: 1-800-348-2227, Ext. 199 or ask for them at your local Christian bookstore.

Persons involved in the occult need to make a good confession to a priest who will hopefully lead them to renounce the evil. The prayer of absolution will help toward deliverance, as well as the power of Holy Communion. If further ministry is needed, the local liaison to the charismatic renewal may be of assistance.

Q My pastor just gave me and some of my friends permission to hold a weekly prayer meeting in the church basement. I've been in the charismatic renewal for a long time, but I've never actually led a prayer meeting. Can you give me any advice on how to go about it?

A The best advice I can give you is to remember that a leader is first of all a servant. As Jesus taught, "Among the Gentiles those who seem to exercise authority lord it over them; their great ones make their importance felt. It cannot be like that with you. Anyone among you who aspires to greatness must serve the rest; whoever wants to rank first among you must serve the needs of all" (Mk 10:42-44).

As a reminder of this, I often refer to myself not as "leader," but as "servant leader." You can fill an important role in your parish if you assume the role of servant, seeking not to be served, but to serve in Christ's name. A recent book by Father Chris Aridas and John Boucher entitled *Bringing Prayer Meetings to Life* (Dove) has a lot of good advice for leaders. You can also call Charismatic Renewal Services (1-800-348-2227, Ext. 199) for their catalog, which lists this book and many other resources for prayer meeting leaders. As you proceed, you may find it helpful to talk to a priest or other lay leaders in your area. They may be able to offer you advice on specific situations based on their experience in charismatic renewal.

Q At my first charismatic prayer meeting, the leader laid hands on me, and I experienced a tremendous surge of power that made me fall backward. Was this the baptism of the Holy Spirit, and if so, how does it differ from being slain in the Spirit?

A I really can't tell you if you've been baptized in the Spirit, but I think I can give you some information that will help you determine that for yourself.

People may be baptized in the Holy Spirit and slain (I prefer "overcome") in the Spirit at the same time, but the physical phenomenon of falling to the floor does not usually accompany being baptized in the Spirit.

Sometimes people are overcome for a moment or two during which time they experience God's love for them, a new peace, or a physical, emotional, or spiritual healing. This experience can be repeated many times without propelling a person forward in the spiritual life. Some people, unfortunately, seek only spiritual sensations, not a deeper relationship with the Lord through the power of the Holy Spirit.

When people are being baptized in the Spirit, however, the

ultimate proof is in whether they are growing (not whether they have attained perfection) in the fruit of the Holy Spirit: "love, joy, peace, patient endurance, kindness, generosity, faith, mildness, and chastity" (Gal 5:22).

Cardinal Leon-Joseph Suenens wrote a book many years ago called *Resting in the Spirit: A Controversial Phenomenon* (Veritas), which gives more information on the subject.

Q Can you recommend any books to help me understand inner healing?

A I recently learned that the book I usually recommend, *Inner Healing* (Paulist), by Father Michael Scanlan, T.O.R., is no longer in print. Even so, I think it would be worthwhile for you to try to obtain it through your local library. Also, Francis MacNutt's book, *Healing* (Ave Maria Press), contains a good chapter on inner healing.

Q Whenever I see someone who has a physical impairment, I always say a prayer for healing for that person. I always expect to see a miracle, yet I never have. Why?

A I commend you for your compassion and your expectant faith.

It is important to respond when the Holy Spirit inspires us to pray for others, but it is also important to leave the results of our prayer in God's hands. We need to pray as Jesus himself taught us, "your will be done" (Mt 6:10). We must have an attitude of humility, trusting that the Lord loves the person with the infirmity more than we do and that he will answer our prayers in his time and his way.

In his book, *Healing* (Ave Maria Press), Francis MacNutt says that we "need to believe in God's healing power and pray for healing, while at the same time realizing that there is a mystery involved and that the person may not be healed." I recommend that you read his book for a balanced view of healing, particularly the chapter entitled, "Eleven Reasons People Are Not Healed."

Q All of the recent troubles in the Catholic charismatic renewal (declining numbers of prayer groups, breakup of covenant communities, and so on) have made me doubt the validity of the whole movement. Has the Church had anything to say about the renewal recently?

A The most recent statement I've come across is the address given by Pope John Paul II to the Council of the International Catholic Charismatic Renewal Office on March 14, 1992. Though warning leaders to make certain the renewal maintains close links with the hierarchy, the Pope says the movement can still contribute much to the Church. Here are some excerpts from that address:

"As you celebrate the twenty-fifth anniversary of the beginning of the Catholic charismatic renewal, I willingly join you in giving praise to God for the many fruits which it has borne in the life of the Church. The emergence of the renewal following the Second Vatican Council was a particular gift of the Holy Spirit to the Church" (No. 1).

"Since the gifts of the Holy Spirit are given for the building up of the Church, you, as leaders of the charismatic renewal, are challenged to seek increasingly effective ways in which the various groups you represent can manifest their complete communion of mind and heart with the Apostolic See and the college of bishops, and cooperate ever more fruitfully in the Church's mission in the world.... Only in this way will the renewal truly serve its ecclesial purpose, helping to ensure that 'the whole body, nourished and knit together through its joints and ligaments, grows with a growth that is from God' (Col 2:19)" (No. 2).

"At this moment in the Church's history, the charismatic renewal can play a significant role in promoting the much-needed defense of Christian life in societies where secularism and materialism have weakened many people's ability to respond to the Spirit and to discern God's loving call. Your contribution to the re-evangelization of society will be made in the first place by personal witness to the indwelling Spirit and by showing forth his presence through works of holiness and solidarity.... To bear witness is to be a powerful leaven among people who perhaps do not fully recognize the value of the salvation that only Jesus Christ can offer" (No. 3).

"The charismatic renewal can also help foster the growth of a solid spiritual life based on the Holy Spirit's power at work in the Church, in the richness of her Tradition, and particularly in her celebration of the sacraments. There can be nó conflict between fidelity to the Spirit and fidelity to the Church and her Magisterium. Whatever shape the charismatic renewal takes — in prayer groups, in covenant communities, in communities of life and service — the sign of its spiritual fruitfulness will always be a strengthening of communion with the universal Church and the local churches" (No. 4, *L'Osservatore Romano*, March 15, 1992).

Chapter IX: Contemporary Issues

Q My wife says she wants to be cremated when she dies and that the Catholic Church now gives this option. I think cremation is still forbidden. Am I right or is she?

A According to the new *Code of Canon Law*, the Church does not "forbid cremation unless it has been chosen for reasons which are contrary to Christian teaching" (Canon 1176). The former ban on cremation had nothing to do with divine or natural law, but with the fact that "it was associated almost exclusively with the aims and the spirit of unbelievers who used cremation to flout and ridicule Christian teaching regarding the immortality of the soul and the resurrection of the body" (*New Catholic Encyclopedia*, Vol. 4, McGraw-Hill).

Despite the lifting of the prohibition on cremation, "the Church earnestly recommends that the pious custom of burying the bodies of the dead be observed" (Canon 1176).

Q What is the Catholic Church's official stance on capital punishment?

A Traditional Catholic teaching holds that the state has the right to inflict capital punishment on any person who is proven guilty of a serious crime. This is rooted in the Old Testament, "If anyone sheds the blood of man, by man shall his blood be shed" (Gn 9:6). The law of the Israelites, at one time or another, listed homicide, bearing false witness in a capital charge, kidnapping, insult or injury to a parent, sexual immorality, witchcraft or magic, idolatry, blasphemy, and sacrilege as capital crimes.

In the age of Christianity, St. Paul defended the right of civil authority when he wrote: "It is not without purpose that the ruler carries the sword; he is God's servant, to inflict his avenging wrath upon the wrongdoer" (Rom 13:4).

The teaching of Jesus, however, would seem to exhort us to waive lawful rights out of love, even for one who sins grievously. "You have heard the commandment 'An eye for an eye, a tooth for a tooth.' But what I say to you is: Offer no resistance to injury. When a person strikes you on the right cheek, turn and offer him the other" (Mt 5:38-39).

Because of Jesus' teaching, the Church cannot but remind the state that it is *not* obliged to exercise its right and that indeed it is better and more humane to rehabilitate the criminal than to inflict vindictive punishment. Considering the sovereignty of God over life, the duty to rehabilitate rather than to avenge, the awareness of human fallibility, the need for reconciliation, and the growing awareness of the complex psychology behind criminal behavior has led to religious and political movements to abolish the death penalty.

Many religious leaders see the need to be consistent in respecting life from the moment of conception to the grave. Some Catholic theologians today teach that the right to life is primordial and inviolable and that the state lacks the right to take it away. This is a legitimate position in the ongoing debate. Many also hold that the death penalty in itself is cruel, unreasonable, and ineffective. Thus on a practical and pastoral level it is acceptable for a Catholic to politically labor for the abolition of the death penalty.

In 1974, the U.S. Catholic Conference declared its opposition to capital punishment. In 1980, the U.S. bishops reaffirmed this commitment to life. The bishops based their position on the moral principle of respect for all human life. They also affirmed three other facts: 1) the death penalty will not deter crime; 2) the death penalty is inequitably administered; and 3) the death penalty will execute innocent people.

The new *Catechism of the Catholic Church* (*Libreria Editrice Vaticana*) upholds the traditional right of the state in crimes of extreme gravity, but Catholics are still free to decide either for abolition or retention of the death penalty.

Q My parish's new youth director started teaching yoga and transcendental meditation techniques to the teenagers in our youth program. He claims there's nothing contradictory to the Catholic faith in this, and says that a Vatican II document even encourages Catholics to learn from non-Christian religions. Is this true?

A Vatican II's "Declaration on the Relation of the Church to Non-Christian Religions" does state that the Catholic Church rejects nothing of what is "true and holy" in other religions and that they "often reflect a ray of that truth which enlightens all men" (No. 2). The document emphasizes, however, that the Church is "in duty bound to proclaim without fail, Christ who is the way, the truth, and the life" and urges us to enter with "*prudence* and charity into discussion and collaboration with members of other religions" (No. 2).

A letter issued in 1989 by the Sacred Congregation for the Doctrine of the Faith (CDF) specifically addresses some aspects of Christian meditation. It affirms that Catholics can take "what is useful from other religions so long as the Christian conception of prayer, its logic, and requirements are never obscured" (No. 16). But, it also reminds us: "Genuine Christian mysticism has nothing to do with technique: It is always a gift of God" (No. 23).

Personally, I've found nothing of use — and a great deal of potential spiritual harm — in the techniques of yoga and transcendental meditation. I advise Catholics not to use these techniques. I am especially against their use with young adults who usually do not possess the level of spiritual maturity nor the educational background necessary to discern "what is useful from other religions." Furthermore, I believe that anyone who has yielded his or her life to Jesus Christ and is in an intimate, loving relationship with him through the Holy Spirit has no need for techniques and practices rooted in non-Christian religions.

As the CDF's letter further states: "From the rich variety of Christian prayer as proposed by the Church, each member of the faithful should seek and find his own way, his own form of prayer. But all of these personal ways, in the end, flow into the *way to the Father*, which is how Jesus Christ has described himself. In the search for his own way, each person will, therefore, let himself be led not so much by his personal tastes as by the Holy Spirit, who guides him, through Christ, to the Father" (No. 29).

For more information on this subject I recommend the booklet *Christians and Yoga?* by Mother Basilea Schlink, the superior of a Lutheran religious order. You can obtain it from the Evangelical Sisterhood of Mary, 9849 N. 40th Street, Phoenix, Arizona 85028; phone: (602) 996-4040. Ralph Martin also deals with the question of integrating non-Christian spiritualities into Christianity in a chapter of his book, *A Crisis of Truth* (Servant). Also, the "Letter to the Bishops of the Catholic Church on Some Aspects of Christian Meditation" quoted above may be ordered from Ignatius Press: (914) 835-4216.

Q My finances got into pretty bad shape over the Christmas season, so I stopped tithing. Now I'm beginning to like the extra cash in my budget. I think I need my money more than the church. Is it really necessary to tithe?

A Nobody tithes because it's easy or enjoyable; we tithe because Scripture says it is proper to tithe. Tithing expresses a fundamental trust in God's provision for our lives. I know many people who have tithed even in times of great financial hardship. They were continually amazed that God could not be out-given. They never became millionaires, but God did indeed supply their needs fully (see Phil 4:19).

According to the teaching of Scripture, tithing is giving at least ten percent of our income to the Church. Although the New Testament does not include specific laws about tithing as does the Old Testament, it does clearly teach that *all* we have actually comes from the Lord's hand and should be submitted to him (see Acts 2:44-45; 4:32-35). The New Testament also teaches that all Christians should support the Church and Christian outreach activities (see Mt 10:10; 1 Cor 9:13-14). In addition to tithing, Christians are also called to share alms with the poor and those in need (see Lk 11:41; Rom 12:8).

I always advise Christians to contribute their tithes to the sources of their spiritual nourishment: their local church first, and then to other Christian ministries and outreaches. We have to seek the Lord about what percentage of our tithe should be offered to our local churches and what percent should go to other ministries. I follow the practice of giving five percent to the local church and five percent to other ministries. As St. Paul wrote, "Everyone must give according to what he has inwardly decided; not sadly, not grudgingly, for God loves a cheerful giver" (2 Cor 9:7).

Q Somehow my name got on a mailing list for anti-Catholic literature . I dismiss most of the tracts as rubbish, but some of them are making me doubt important aspects of Catholic doctrine. Have you ever received anti-Catholic tracts?

A I understand how upset and concerned you are over the anti-Catholic literature you've received. When I was the host of Catholic television and radio shows, I often received anti-Catholic tracts and comic books. They invariably consisted of distortions of Catholic teachings. I usually throw out any materials I get from anti-Catholic organizations and intercede for the people who printed and sent them, asking God to change their hearts and cause them to repent.

The people who send such materials are obviously unaware of the authentic teachings of the Catholic Church, which are rooted in Sacred Scripture and Tradition handed down from the apostles. These tracts are usually slanderous and are certainly not inspired by the Holy Spirit or rooted in the truth. Such attacks upon the Church only lead to confusion and contribute to the lack of unity among Christians.

You might want to write to Catholic Answers, a large apologetics and evangelization organization, for their catalog. They sell many books, tapes, and tracts that explain the Catholic faith and answer questions about the Church that are raised by anti-Catholics. Their address is: P.O. Box 17490, San Diego, California 92177. I also recommend Dr. Alan Schreck's book *Catholic and Christian* (Servant).

Q I am a news reporter for a small market radio station. Sometimes I get caught up in getting a news story without regard to how it may affect the people involved. How can I bring Christ into my work while providing news and information to the people of my community?

A Too often the media forgets that its job is to serve the common good, not just to get good ratings. I'm happy to hear you want to provide timely, accurate information to your listeners and also want to uphold the human dignity of those in the news.

Vatican II's "Decree on the Means of Social Communication" (*Inter Mirifica*) and the 1971 "Pastoral Instruction on the Means of Social Communication" (*Communio et Progressio*) recognize that this is no easy task, yet encourage the media to responsibly and truthfully communicate to their fellow men.

"Since the media of social communication are for mankind, communicators should be consumed by the desire to serve men. They can only achieve this if they really do know and love their fellow man. The more communicators remember that beyond the lifeless instruments which pass on their words and images are countless living men and women, the more satisfaction they will get from their work and the better they will help others" (*Communio et Progressio*, No. 72).

The document urges "the active cooperation of Christians who are professionally competent in this field," calling it "a major service to social communication" (No. 103).

The instruction notes, however, and calls others to realize, that all communicators, Christians and non-Christians, have limitations just like the rest of us: "The recipients of information should have a clear conception of the predicament of those that purvey information. They should not look for a superhuman perfection in the communicators" (No. 41).

Nonetheless, communicators must strive to make their communications "comply with certain essential requirements, and these are sincerity, honesty, and truthfulness. Good intentions and a clear conscience do not thereby make a communication sound and reliable. A communication must state the truth. It must accurately reflect the situation with all its implications" (No. 17).

"The right to information is not limitless," the instruction further states. "It has to be reconciled with other existing rights. There is the right of truth which guards the good name both of men and of societies. There is the right of privacy which protects the private life of families and individuals.... Indeed, whenever public good is at stake, discretion and discrimination and careful judgment should be used in the preparation of news" (No. 42).

This is not easy because "Communicators must hold the wandering attention of a harried and hurried public by vivid reporting. And yet they must not give way to the temptation of making the news sensational in such a way that they risk distorting it by taking it out of context or by exaggerating it out of all proportion" (No. 40).

Whenever the media makes errors or exaggerates reports, the audience has "a right and duty to expect ... that a rapid and clear correction should follow any mistake or misrepresentation that has found its way into a report" (No. 41).

I recommend that you study both documents on social communications as well as the more recent papal addresses on the media. I'm sure that by informing your conscience and daily asking the Lord for the guidance of his Holy Spirit you will be well-equipped to make right judgments about the problems you face on the job.

Q Does the Catholic Church have an official approach to hypnosis as a means of healing?

A The Church's official approach is one of caution. Many clinicians and moralists believe that hypnosis is of little value as a therapeutic agent. In very limited cases, the Church approves of its use, but then only when it is administered in a clinical situation by a competent and upright physician or psychologist who is aware of its abuses and dangers. If it is not administered correctly, hypnosis can result in physical, psychological, physiological, and spiritual harm.

In light of the significant abuses and dangers connected to hypnosis, my pastoral approach is to discourage its use in any situation. God does not intend for us to surrender control of our human consciousness to anyone other than Jesus, who is our Lord and healer. Instead, I advise people to use the channels of God's healing that are available in the Church through the sacraments, pastoral counseling, and legitimate forms of psychotherapy that respect faith. Those in need of healing should seek the ongoing support of a loving body of Christians, competent Christian counseling, and direct prayer for healing.

Q Every month Jehovah's Witnesses come knocking on our door. I don't want to be impolite, but when I let them talk to me I get confused. I know they are not right, but I'm not good at arguing. What can I do?

A The Jehovah's Witnesses are not Christians, although they may present themselves as Christians. They do not believe that Jesus is actually God, nor do they believe in the Holy Spirit as the third person of the Trinity. Jehovah's Witnesses attempt to lead people away from the truth of salvation in Jesus Christ.

You do not need to invite Jehovah's Witnesses into your home to listen to their ideas. You should feel free to inform them that you are a Catholic Christian, that you do not accept their religion, and that you are not interested in listening to their ideas or receiving any of their literature.

If you'd like to be able to defend your faith next time they come, write to Catholic Answers, P.O. Box 17490, San Diego, California 92177. Their catalog has many books, pamphlets, and audio and video tapes listed, which explain the beliefs and missionary tactics of Jehovah's Witnesses and other sects.

Q May Catholics join the Freemasons?

A Catholics who joined Masonic societies were once excommunicated, but that penalty was not repeated in the 1983 *Code of Canon Law*. However, Canon 1374 allows a local bishop to impose a sanction on those who join any association that works against the Church.

In some countries, the Masons are viewed as merely a fraternal, philanthropic order; in others they are openly anticlerical and hostile to the Catholic Church. More important than the question of whether Masons work against the Church is the question of whether its principles conflict with Catholic Church teaching.

On November 26, 1983, the Sacred Congregation for the Doctrine of the Faith published a declaration indicating that Catholics joining the Masons are involved in serious sin and are to be barred from the Eucharist. This strong stance indicates that the principles of Freemasonry are incompatible with the disciplines and doctrines of the Catholic Church. Furthermore, a lengthy report from a committee of the United States Catholic Conference of Bishops issued in June 1985 calls Freemasonry "irreconcilable" with Catholic Christianity and describes the "politically reactionary and racist" nature of most U.S. Masonry.

My simple pastoral answer to your question would be that Catholics should not join the Masons. If an individual does not accept my position, I would advise him to consult with his local bishop.

Q Before I became a Christian, astrology was a big part of my life. Now I just read the horoscopes in the newspaper for fun, but I've been wondering if even that much involvement is too much. What do you think?

A I am happy to hear that you have accepted Christ. I believe you should completely cut your ties with astrology and renounce such activity.

I feel strongly that Christians should avoid any involvement — even a minimal one — with astrology. Scripture (see Is 47:12-15) and the teachings of the early Church clearly indicate that astrology (as contrasted with the scientific study of astronomy) is a pseudoscience that cannot lead to salvation. The Lord does not intend for us to direct our lives according to astrological signs; the only "sign" Christians should live under is the sign of the cross.

I encourage you, in the words of St. Paul, to "lay aside your former way of life and the old self which deteriorates through illusion and desire, and acquire a fresh, spiritual way of thinking" and to "put on that new man created in God's image, whose justice and holiness are born of truth" (Eph 4:22-24).

Q It's my understanding that gambling is a sin. If so, why do Catholic parishes sponsor bingo and other games of chance?

A Gambling is not intrinsically evil and can be an acceptable form of entertainment.

The *New Catholic Encyclopedia* (Vol. 6, McGraw-Hill) has an excellent article on gambling, which says that it can be sinful when "a person has no right to risk the money he bets, either because it is not his own, or because he needs it for the support of his family or for the discharge of other obligations." The article also notes that gambling is sinful when the gambler knows "the person with whom he bets ought not to risk his money."

I am not opposed to recreational bingo for senior citizens, but I regret that bingo, Las Vegas nights, and the like have to be used to support church ministries and institutions. Even though it is not evil in itself, church-sponsored gambling scandalizes those who believe it to be sinful, and for their sakes, I think we have to try to "avoid any semblance of evil" (1 Thes 5:22). If I were ever responsible for parish fundraising, I would attempt to wean the people from gambling. I would encourage them to start tithing so that such support would not be needed.

Compulsive gambling is an illness and can be treated. A person with this addiction should avoid gambling, even recreational gambling.

Q I have a friend who was once involved in satanic activity. She recently became a Catholic, but she says she has no ability to concentrate at Mass or while praying the Rosary. Could she still be under satanic influence?

A From your letter it is hard to determine if satanic activity is the cause of your friend's inability to concentrate. It is possible that she could still be under occult bondage if she has not been adequately ministered to by way of the sacrament of reconciliation and prayer for deliverance. But there could be other causes for the problem you describe, or a combination of spiritual, emotional, and physical causes.

If the woman herself believes that the root of her problem is spiritual, she should seek out her local diocesan liaison for the Catholic charismatic renewal for counsel. He may be able to help her discern the cause of her difficulty, and if necessary, help her locate a priest or lay team who understand the ministry of healing and deliverance and whose ministries have borne the test of time.

In the meantime, she should make a complete confession of her life to a prayerful priest and in his presence renounce all satanic or occult activity. I also recommend that she participate regularly, if not daily, in the Eucharist. The power to free her may be experienced in the sacrament of reconciliation and in receiving Holy Communion.

Q With Halloween fast approaching, I am again faced with the dilemma of whether or not to let my grammar-school-aged children go out trick or treating. What do you think about Halloween celebrations?

A Don't assume that you have to celebrate Halloween according to today's secular customs. As a matter of fact, I usually advise parents to celebrate All Saints' Day (November 1), which honors the Lord and all the holy men and women who have gone on before us, instead of the distorted version of All Hallows Eve, which unfortunately has come to honor Satan, death, and evil spirits.

Some families I know get together for All Saints' Day parties. The children dress up as saints they admire and each has a chance to tell a little bit about the life of his or her saint. These parties are replete with games and treats, so the children don't feel cheated when they compare their "haul" with their peers at school. I believe that it is more appropriate to celebrate in this way than to follow contemporary Halloween customs.

Q As the year 2000 approaches, I've been hearing more and more interpretations of the Book of Revelation. Most of them are contradictory. What does the Catholic Church teach about this?

A I think this subject is too broad and complex to address here. I recommend a book called *The Apocalypse: Understanding the Book of Revelation and the End of the World* (Servant) by Father George Montague, S.M. His commentary gives a balanced perspective on Revelation and what it teaches on the end of the world and provides a useful bibliography for those interested in further study.

Father Montague is a professor of Sacred Scripture at St. Mary's University in San Antonio, Texas. He has written many books and is a frequent contributor to *New Covenant*.

Index

A

B

C

E

Easter 55
Eucharist (eucharistic) 10, 11, 17, 19, 20-21, 23, 32, 37, 39, 40, 52-53, 61, 63, 70, 72-73, 77, 87, 88, 115, 117 *see also* Communion, Real Presence, Table of the Lord
evangelization (evangelist) 25, 59, 61, 70, 91
excommunication 32, 33, 34, 42, 114
extraordinary minister 40

F

family life 80
fasting 93-94
Father, use of 41-42
fathers of the Church 42
feasts 55
forgiveness 9, 10, 14, 16, 18, 21, 29, 31, 45
Franciscan University 6, 22, 41
Freemasons 114 *see also* Masons
fundamentalist 67-68
funeral 23, 69, 70, 75

G

Gabriel (angel) 69
gambling 116
General Instruction on the Roman Missal 11, 20
"General Norms for the Liturgical Year and the Calendar" 56
Good Friday 94
guilt 25, 26, 31, 71, 79, 80, 106

H

Halloween 117-118
healing 10, 13-14, 17, 37, 66, 98, 99, 102, 103, 113, 117

K

L

M

masturbation 78-80
media 37, 111-113
Mediatrix 67-68 *see also* Blessed Virgin Mary; Mary; Mother of
  God
memorials 55
Michael (archangel) 69
miracle 48, 50, 103
moral relativism 25
morality 32, 80, 86
Morning Prayer 60
mortal sin 18, 21 *see also* sin
Mother of God 88, 91 *see also* Blessed Virgin Mary; Mary;
  Mediatrix
Mulieris Dignitatem 39

N

National Conference of Catholic Bishops 94
natural family planning 86, 88
New American Bible 62
New Covenant (magazine) 54, 118
New International Version (bible) 62
New Jerusalem Bible 62
New Testament 13, 20, 23, 24, 60, 61, 66, 69, 79, 94, 98, 110
Newman, Blessed John Henry 95
novenas 58

O

obscene language 30-31
occult 101, 117
Office of Readings 60
Old Testament 20, 61, 66, 69, 106, 110
"On Reserving Priestly Ordination to Men Alone" (*Ordinatio
  Sacerdotalis*) 38
"On the Regulation of Birth" (*Humanae Vitae*) 85-87

R

Raphael (archangel) 69
Real Presence of the Lord 20 *see also* Communion, Eucharist, Table of the Lord
"Reality of Life After Death, The" 76
reconciliation 10, 14, 16, 21, 25, 34, 42, 107, 117 *see also* confession; penance
Redemptoris Missio 51-52
relics 92
religious 37, 40-41, 43, 52, 86, 109
religious education 40
renewal 18, 39, 45, 50, 70, 98, 101-102, 104-105, 117
repentance 14, 34, 37, 93
Resurrection (of Christ) 15, 16, 47, 55, 56, 68, 76
resurrection 75, 106
Revelation (Book of) 118
revelation 34-35, 59, 74
right to life 107
Rite of Penance of the Roman Ritual 18
role of women 39
Roman Rite 90
Rome 43, 47, 69, 74
Rosary 58-59, 60, 100, 116

S

sacramentals 90
sacraments 9, 19, 21, 42, 53, 88, 90, 105, 113
Sacred Congregation for the Doctrine of the Faith 76, 78, 82, 88, 108, 115
saints 30-31, 39, 42, 45, 47, 55-56, 69-70, 88, 92, 117
salt (sacred) 89
salvation 14, 18, 19-20, 33, 35, 64-65, 72, 74, 90, 96, 98, 100, 105, 114, 115
Satan 43, 50, 101, 116-117

Tradition 7, 15, 35, 44
tradition 22, 33, 38, 42, 43, 61, 69, 78, 80, 90, 93
transcendental meditation 108-109
transubstantiation 72-73
Trinity 9, 95, 114
tubal ligation 31

V

Vatican II 13, 17, 43, 58, 60, 67, 85, 91, 108, 111 *see also* Second
  Vatican Council
vernacular 43
virginity 46

W

Way of the Cross 58-59
weekdays 55, 94
women priests 38-40
women's ordination 39

Y

yielding 99
yoga 108, 109
youth 40, 71, 100, 108